Demystifying Mediumship

What makes a medium?

Kerry Alderuccio

Published November 2021

ISBN: 978-0-6453072-0-7

www.kerryalderuccio.com

A copy of this publication can be found in the National Library of Australia.
Edited by The Manuscript Agency, Katoomba, NSW.
Designed and typeset by Bec Yule @ Red Chilli Design
Printed by Ingram Book Printing

DEDICATION

*To my son, Sam, and father, Jim Bell, this book
is for you. Your combined spiritual presence is a
reassuring constant in my life and in my work
as a medium.*

*Through accepting reality, I'm forced to appreciate
that life and death go hand in hand, and you
cannot have one without the other. But the
connections remain forever.*

*To each and every contributor, I give thanks for
allowing me to share your deeply personal and often
confronting stories. Your openness and honesty
in finding your own pathway to mediumship
is as varied as it is extraordinary.*

*A special thank you to Anne-Marie Bond,
who allowed me to use her wonderful spirit
artwork on the cover.*

CONTENTS

PREFACE

In my mid-fifties I made a discovery that most people never make: a new ability presented itself, and this previously untapped skill was mediumship. It took the sudden and tragic death of our much-loved nineteen-year-old son, Sam, to awaken my latent gift. I now know that many mediums find a tragedy or trauma is the catalyst for this revelation.

I wrote my first book, *A Mother's Journey: a story of everlasting love and evidence of life after death*, in 2017, five years after Sam's passing in a car accident. After losing Sam, I was desperate to find books that explained 'death' properly. The concept of death being the final act of life never sat well with me and was not what I ever believed or accepted. No adequate books on the subject were forthcoming, so I wrote my own.

My understanding of death differed completely to what was offered in most of the books I read. Within me was an innate knowing that death meant 'life after life', and that was where my interest lay. I chose a different path that I knew nothing about, but I knew that my answer would be found there. I had been communicating quietly and privately with Sam since the day of the accident. This came easily and naturally for me, and I naively assumed that everyone spoke to their loved ones in the same way. I began to explore mediumship, and after my first session with a medium, another world opened up, and I began a journey of no return.

With much self-discovery, I found and subsequently embraced my own mediumistic abilities, and life took another turn. I didn't expect the reaction from family, friends and strangers when I started working as a practising medium. The attitudes varied from acceptance, complete scepticism, mixed curiosity, mild fascination and everything in between. I also encountered pity; I believe some people misconstrued a mental breakdown due to Sam's death.

I constantly heard the words, 'You don't look like a medium; you seem so normal!' Having many friends who are also mediums, I knew I needed more than my own story to better explain what mediumship is and ultimately to attempt to demystify the many myths and misconceptions that surround it. I wanted to hear what others had to say, so through invitation and kind acceptance, seventeen fellow mediums and friends have bared their souls and shared their own stories.

INTRODUCTION

Every wonderful contributor was already known to me personally; most I knew very well, and others were relatively new friends. Many of these people I met at the Arthur Findlay College in the United Kingdom, either as tutors or fellow students. They have highly diverse backgrounds: they are of both sexes, varying age groups and from a number of different countries. Each has an incredible story to tell.

Initially, I was concerned that the mini biographies might sound too generic, and I didn't want seventeen different people saying the same thing. What I didn't anticipate was the raw emotion that has been openly shared in these incredible stories. I knew certain aspects about my friends, but I had no concept of the personal struggles that have touched many of their lives. There are divorces, substance abuse, financial disasters, struggles with sexuality, battles with alcoholism, heartbreaking family losses, entrapment in the Jehovah's Witnesses Church and breakdowns requiring hospitalisation.

By sharing these personal journeys in life, I aim to allow you to appreciate that each and every medium has experienced completely different ways of discovering and embracing their gifts. Not everyone was actively seeking mediumship, and one experienced it initially as an unwelcome intrusion into her life. The one factor that is apparent for all is that mediumship presented itself at a time when they needed to find it.

Mediumship is hard to explain and is often totally misunderstood, so in simple language, I have endeavoured to explain this ancient practice. It was essential to make some attempt to also demystify much of the unnecessary and unwarranted hype that often surrounds mediumship. Understanding the basic mechanics of mediumship will hopefully allow you to gain a broader knowledge of what takes place during a sitting and to appreciate the healing aspects of a mediumship reading.

For the curious, I hope you will discover and learn much from what is shared in these chapters. It is my belief that too often subtle personal contacts with the spirit world are missed or dismissed. As humans, we put too many magical moments down to coincidence or imagination, thereby depriving ourselves of what they really are: beautiful spiritual encounters with your own loved ones. Some of the wonderful examples within will hopefully spark past memories for you.

I know some readers may be disillusioned with their own spiritual development to date, and hopefully a clearer and more realistic approach will be found here. It's important to also stress that this book isn't just for mediums, psychics and healers; it is for anyone and everyone who loves reading about the lives of others.

Like myself, many mediums hear the words, 'You don't look the type!' Please know, there is no type. Just as it's impossible to tell in a crowd of strangers who's good at playing the piano, driving a city bus or performing open heart surgery, mediums won't stand out, and we walk among you daily, in that very same crowd of strangers.

Chapter one

WHAT IS MEDIUMSHIP?

Mediumship is a natural communication between the living and the dead … that's it! As far as explanations go, this one doesn't begin to answer anything at all, but it is still the answer.

The role of a medium is hard to define. It's difficult to explain, and those people who don't believe in an afterlife find it impossible to decipher. If you don't believe that the spirit world exists, then undoubtedly you won't accept that mediumship is right, real or remotely credible.

There are two main patterns of thought regarding what happens when we die. Some of the world's population believe that death is final and absolute. It is the end of life's road, and your existence is now completely over and fully finished; you are extinguished. Within this group, the notion of ongoing communication with the deceased is ridiculous, as that person no longer exists, and they are now nothing but an empty shell. This is an extremely bleak outlook in my opinion and certainly not one that has ever been in my own belief system.

I'm of the opposing group; I believe that life goes on after a physical death takes place. I've always thought that way, and I came to this conclusion as a very young child. It's an inherent understanding that I have always had. It's not a religious one, and it wasn't thrust or forced upon me in any way; it comes from a place of 'knowing'.

It is not my intention to try to change anyone's personal perspectives, as the subject of death is understandably unpalatable for most and (sadly) not something that is talked about openly. Through my own experiences as a medium, I now have a much greater personal understanding of what happens when we die, and as a result my own death doesn't frighten me. I accept death as a part of the cycle of life: birth, life and death. But may I add that losing a loved one is the most confronting, raw and painful experience that any of us will ever have to endure, and sadly, we will all lose more than one special person during our lifetimes.

At this juncture, I would like to share some hopefully helpful and very simple explanations of mediumship. Mediums can and do play a part in the healing process following the passing of a loved one. Our role is to provide a calming and natural communication between the deceased person (spirit communicator) and the sitter/recipient (person having the reading); we are the bridge between the spirit world and this one.

Without dwelling on the engineering of the communication, put simply, mediumship is the ability to sense the presence of spirit and be able to communicate with spirit souls and share what they want to express. This communication doesn't take place in the same way that we converse with the living; with mediumship it happens on a completely different level altogether. It is the soul of the spirit and the medium's own soul that connect during a mediumship reading, and that is how the communication takes place.

To explain this better, imagine a small ball of energy, a vibrant spark of light that resides just above your navel, in your torso. This spark of light is your soul. The soul doesn't live in your brain or heart, as is often assumed; the human soul is located in the middle of your body. When the medium is communicating with the spirit world, they are connecting from their own soul to the soul energy of the communicator in the spirit world.

The medium's role is to relay everything, exactly as it is received, without changing any aspect of what is shared. Some of the information given will sound strange and maybe ridiculous, but the evidence is for the recipient and not for the medium. The medium should never filter or process what they receive through their brain; it must only ever be from soul to soul, as the human brain is likely to misinterpret and change what was received in order for it to make sense to the medium. It never matters if the medium doesn't understand the information being shared, but it's vital that the recipient does.

To give an example of unintentionally distorting what was being communicated, I once did a reading for a young woman, where I was communicating with her grandmother in spirit. I heard the word 'Ireland', and my brain immediately got in the way and I assumed that my sitter's grandmother must be of Irish ancestry. She couldn't accept what I said as being correct, and rightly so; I was completely wrong, and she had no connection to Ireland at all. What I heard was actually the word 'island', and if I had just shared this, without allowing my brain to make geographical assumptions, it would have made complete sense, because her grandmother lived on an actual island!

Though this book was not written specifically about the techniques or mechanics of mediumship, I believe it's important to have some understanding of how mediums communicate and receive information from spirit. During a mediumship reading, all mediums use a number of senses, known as 'clairs'. Most mediums will attune to at least one or more of these senses, and the main ones are clairvoyance (sight), clairaudience (sound), clairscent (smell), clairgustance (taste), clairsentience (feeling) and clairempathy (emotion).

In order for a reading to unfold properly and for it to be successful to both the sitter and the spirit communicator, the medium must be able to identify very early on who they are communicating with. Are they with a male or female spirit, and what is the relationship between the spirit and the sitter? Once these vital aspects are identified and confirmed, the memories and shared experiences can be brought forward and verified, because the sitter knows who is communicating with them.

The strongest connections are usually made through clairsentience and clairvoyance, as these clairs allow the medium to verbalise what they 'see' and 'feel' from the spirit. The true essence of the spirit communicator can be felt when receiving information this way, and the medium can visually describe past memories, places and shared experiences. Their clairempathy will allow the medium to share the intensity of what these emotions evoke in the spirit communicator, which will in turn touch the emotions of the sitter.

There are a number of different types of mediumship readings, with the two predominant ones being one-on-one sittings and platform demonstrations. Both will be explored here, as each of the contributors share their personal stories. The one-on-one sitting is just that; it is a reading given by the medium to one other person, in a private setting. The medium makes contact with one or more spirit communicators, and the sitter validates or rejects each piece of evidence being given via the medium. It is a beautiful way to reconnect loved ones and invariably evokes both healing and hope for the sitter.

With a platform demonstration, the medium is often literally on a raised platform, with an audience in attendance. These types of readings may take place in a Spiritualist church, private hall, auditorium, private home or anywhere at all. During a platform demonstration, the medium connects with a spirit communicator, and they share the information they receive with the audience. The medium will either be guided by spirit directly to the correct recipient in the audience, or they may ask the audience if anyone present can understand the information they shared. Once the initial evidence is confirmed as factual and relevant to a particular person, the medium then works solely with them, delivering piece after piece of information, which are either confirmed or rejected by the recipient. It's incredible to witness this type of reading, especially when it's done with an experienced medium. Even though it is performed with an audience in attendance, the healing power of the spirit contact is just as great.

With both types of readings, it is essential to note that it is the spirit who decides who comes through during the communication, and they will also determine what they wish to share. It is never the medium who decides what is said: the medium is there to be of service to the spirit world; the spirit world is not present to be of service to the medium. This is an important lesson for every medium and sitter to appreciate.

Strangely, there are certain rules that need to be explained by the medium before a reading of any kind. Conversely to what many people think, the medium does not want to know a single piece of information about who the sitter is hoping to connect with. They don't want names, ages, relationships, occupations, hobbies or anything at all. What the medium does require from the sitter is a simple 'yes', 'no' or 'I don't understand' answer to each piece of information that is given, so they know what is being said makes sense, or not. Nothing is to be elaborated on by the sitter, as that additional information may come out later on in the reading.

A reading will always be disappointing for the sitter if they have a predetermined list of subjects and information they expect to be covered during the sitting. These may be of relevance and importance to them, but they are rarely what the spirit communicator wants to express. Sadly, this can leave the sitter feeling both frustrated and disappointed with the reading, and the medium and spirit communicator are likely to feel the same way. A mediumship reading is the spirit's opportunity to share what's important for them to convey to their loved one, and sometimes this may be at odds with sitters' preconceived expectations.

I once did a reading for a bereaved parent who wouldn't accept that I had their child in spirit present, purely because the child didn't communicate the things they expected them to share. This parent wanted to hear very specific information, and anything less meant that the reading, in their eyes, had failed. Without knowing a single piece of information about my sitter, I brought through the fact that they had lost a child. I had the right sex, the right initial of their first name, the exact age when they passed, how they died, specific information regarding their state of mind pre- death, correct information about living siblings and their previous passions in life. This spirit child was desperately trying to express what they needed their parent to know. The parent was denying their very existence, based purely on the child not sharing exactly what they had wanted and expected them to say. When this happens, it is so sad.

As mentioned, the medium doesn't decide which spirits make their presence known at a reading, and occasionally the spirit present is not expected, or indeed welcome. Once during a private sitting, a spirit came through and when I identified who they were, my sitter was openly shocked and disappointed, as they were hoping for someone else. Some spirits come through because they want to offer apologies for situations that took place when they lived. These types of readings are always very emotional but also extremely cathartic and healing for both the sitter and no doubt for the spirit communicator too. In this particular instance, it was a father in spirit, who had a long-term and painful rift with his son, and it was confronting and overwhelming for my client to have his father seek forgiveness for his past actions.

For the uninitiated, there is often confusion about the different names that are used by the people who do the readings, and this can cause problems, with sitters potentially seeing the wrong type of reader. Psychic and mediumship readings are not the same thing, and it's important to have an understanding of what mediums and psychics do, as the two types of readings are very different.

Mediums have a special ability to connect and communicate with the energy of the spirit world, and they are also able to read the energy of living people, so they are often called psychic mediums, or just mediums. On the other hand, psychics are not able to communicate with the spirit world, but they can read the energy of living people by using Tarot, Angel or Oracle cards, tea leaves, crystal balls or by using nothing at all. Psychics can and do provide meaningful guidance to the sitter during a reading, and just like mediumship, each piece of information is validated or rejected as the reading unfolds. When I do psychic readings for clients, I use Tarot cards to talk about the sitter's past, present and future, and I answer specific questions by reading their energy.

Why do people seek out mediums? It's an interesting question and one that has many possible explanations but only one true answer: to reconnect with a loved one in the spirit world. The outcome of a successful mediumship reading will create a real sense of peace and healing for the sitter and spirit alike. Sadly, society in many cultures has conditioned the vast majority of the population to believe that communication with the dead is somehow barbaric, anti-religious and misguided. This is a tragic misconception and one I have never understood. I don't understand why humanity is so willing to deny spirit and their loved ones, the opportunity to be 'seen', 'heard' and 'felt' again, with the help of a medium.

Chapter two

Discovering my mediumship

My first introduction to mediumship was an exceptional reading with a wonderful woman called Lorraine Culross, in Melbourne's south-eastern suburbs. It was just six weeks after Sam's passing. Lorraine's reading yielded not only incredible insight and evidence of Sam's ongoing existence, his 'life after life', it also provided a form of healing that was so strong it was almost tangible. Thankfully, my husband, Sergio, was with me, and through Lorraine's skills as a medium, she brought Sergio, Sam and me all back together again. Although it was only for an hour, it did happen, and it was very real.

During the reading, Lorraine spoke briefly about her own daughter having mediumship abilities and how she always longed to have the same but felt that she didn't. Lorraine shared with us what her turning point was for her own gifts to finally become apparent and this made me wonder, can mediumship happen for everyone who wants it?

I've always believed that spirits live on; this had been a lifelong and instinctive reality for me but not something I'd ever discussed widely with anyone. Until our reading with Lorraine I didn't know that complete strangers could somehow make meaningful and evidential contact with the spirit world. Through the evidence that was given by Lorraine, it was clear that Sam's soul had survived his physical death and he was now in the afterlife, just as I had hoped and always believed.

My need to explore mediumship for myself was all-consuming, and in 2014 I joined a spiritual circle and began a personal exploration into the world of psychics, mediums and healers that took me to the Arthur Findlay College in the United Kingdom. Through my yearly visits, entailing ongoing mediumship tuition and training, I have met and made friends with many wonderful and gifted mediums at the college, many of whom share their stories in the following chapters.

Growing up, I had absolutely no concept of what mediums or psychics were. I didn't know any friends who saw mediums, and I had never had a reading of any kind until Sam passed. Looking back now it seems odd, because throughout my life and from a very early age I have been acutely aware of the changes I felt in the energy around me. In bed at night I could feel the closeness of unseen beings in my bedroom, and occasionally I saw dark shapes moving about in the room from the safety of my bed. For some reason I was neither frightened nor saw the need to share this information with my parents, sister or anyone else. At school I was outwardly no different, but I was always deeply sensitive to the emotions of others, and I would somehow know information instinctively without having been told.

Premonitions for me happened regularly, and I accepted this ability without questioning it. I have always had a knowing that life is much more than what we see with our own eyes or can comprehend with our limited and sometimes one-dimensional minds. The concept of 'life after death' was always very real, and the thought of actual 'death' remained totally inconceivable to me. To my way of thinking, that small inner voice within me could never be extinguished. Nothing could turn it off; it was the essence of my own soul, and it would remain forever. I was about five years old when I came to these conclusions.

As an adult, our little family consisted of my husband, Sergio, our children Carla and Sam, two cats, Jingles and Megan, and me. Home was in the suburb of Flemington in Melbourne, famous for having the racetrack where the Melbourne Cup is run and won every November. We raised our children with all the normal expectations, dance lessons, music classes, tennis coaching, footy and cricket matches for Sam and soccer games for Carla, countless birthday parties and sleepovers for both. Carla and Sam attended kindergarten at St Brendan's and primary school at Flemington Primary, which were just up the street. Secondary school was at Wesley College on St Kilda Road, a tram and train trip away, or, on a good day, a lift with Mum. Life was great … until it wasn't.

On a cold, wet and miserable day on 3 May 2012, Sam and two of his mates, Raph and Jesse, passed away together in a horrific car accident on Westgarth Street in the suburb of Northcote. Our family car, a parked vehicle and a large tree were all involved in the fatal crash, and Sam was at the wheel. All three boys died at the scene, and the car was engulfed by fire. The police had the impossible task of sharing this news with three unsuspecting families, and the world as we all knew it stopped spinning and life came crashing down.

From that moment onwards nothing seemed within my control, including the overpowering spiritual presence of Sam, which was immediate and strong. Sam's spirit had barely left us only hours beforehand, yet after arriving home from the Northcote police station I felt his energy, his love, his closeness, his support; he was truly still there, and I desperately needed to know how I could somehow get closer to him. Feeling Sam around me was truly comforting and reassuring, but it was also something that remained my secret. How could I explain to Sergio and Carla what was happening when I couldn't explain it to myself?

Through the help of Google, and I believe also divine intervention, I joined a spiritual development circle that was run by Toni Reilly, a wonderful woman, a teacher and now a close friend. I had no idea what a development circle was, but nevertheless I found myself there, and I was in the right place. I could cry freely among this small group of complete strangers; they all knew my story about Sam, and everyone was extremely considerate and kind. Toni introduced me to meditation, which I found incredibly easy to do, and the clarity, direction and peace I received from each of the meditations was beyond my imagination. Sam was with me each and every time when I meditated, and I found I could communicate freely with him in this very natural way. The emotional impact of 'being together' again was truly enormous, and each meditation always ended in happy tears.

I have no idea what Sergio and Carla thought took place at my weekly circle group, but they knew I enjoyed whatever I was doing there. I'm sure there were some slight or perhaps major concerns when I started using various pendulums and Tarot cards at home, but thankfully neither questioned my mental state nor tried to prevent me from pursuing this path. At least I was honest with them both in what I was doing, even if it wasn't completely clear to me at that point why I was embracing such strange and new practices.

Each week at circle we did many types of psychic exercises, and I surprised myself at being able to read Tarot cards easily and with unexpected accuracy. My personal communications continued with Sam, but we didn't do any mediumship readings for one another at circle; they were only psychic ones. I had experienced a wonderful second reading with my original medium, Lorraine, and Sam was again present sharing all sorts of evidence that Lorraine couldn't possibly know about. I found the whole concept of mediumship remarkable, and something deep within made me want to see if I had any mediumship abilities as well. I knew I was a psychic, but could I be a psychic medium? I knew that Toni was both a psychic and a medium, so I asked her how she trained to communicate with the spirit world. Toni shared three life-changing words with me: 'Arthur Findlay College'.

I went home and researched the college as much as I could, and what I read excited me beyond belief. This training school for psychics, mediums and healers was in the United Kingdom and had been operating since the mid-1960s. Thankfully, I had Sergio and Carla's blessing to explore my own mediumship capabilities, though I'm not truly sure they really knew what that entailed, or what the college actually taught. My first trip to Arthur Findlay College was in early 2015, and it was then I discovered that I had mediumistic abilities. I've attended every year since for a fortnight of classes, until Covid-19 closed the college temporarily in 2020 and 2021.

After learning about my latent abilities I began very slowly performing readings from home for friends and strangers. Initially, I was more comfortable with doing just psychic readings using Tarot cards, and as my confidence grew I began to do mediumship readings as well. It is preferable and easier to read for a complete stranger, which may sound counterintuitive; no pun intended! Once you know anything at all about the sitter, your job becomes more difficult. Reading for friends is something I have done, but it is more challenging because you are constantly referencing what you already know about them and their loved one in spirit.

Even though my mediumship wasn't apparent to me until Sam passed, I do believe it was always present within me; it just wasn't necessary to discover it until then. Being a medium is not possible for everyone, but I do believe that everyone can have very real personal mediumistic experiences with their own loved ones in spirit though they can't communicate successfully with the spirit world for other people, which is what defines a medium.

It saddens me when I speak to people who have experienced these beautiful personal mediumistic communications, but they are in denial of what actually took place. A number of factors will spoil the magic of these moments, including long-held instilled beliefs and religious constraints that tell them it's impossible. The result is blindly accepting that it can't be true or happening and they must be imagining it. When spirits communicate and impress their presence on a living person it is a very gentle and extremely subtle communication that is often missed. The uninitiated often expect something much more conclusive and earth-shattering when connecting with spirit energy, and it doesn't happen in that way.

When I wrote my first book about Sam's passing and what I experienced afterwards, I did so for a number of reasons. I couldn't find a book that spoke frankly about dealing with the confrontation of an unexpected death, and everything I did read seemed so generic, clinical and heartless. Nothing provided answers for me. I wanted to hear real stories written by actual grieving parents; I had so many questions, and the answers were elusive to non-existent. By writing and sharing my own story I know I not only helped myself to heal in many ways, but I realise too that I also enabled Sergio and Carla to understand more about what happens when someone dies, and how the connection between the two worlds can never be broken.

I am aware that many of my clients have come to me because they too have had to endure the pure agony of losing a child. Because I have walked that road myself, I know the absolute pain that cannot and should not be met with empty phrases like, 'Time will heal', 'It's God's way' and unbelievably, 'Are you over it yet?' These pointless statements do nothing but accentuate the total lack of understanding around what grieving parents go through. When I meet these bereaved parents we rarely know one another, but we certainly do understand each other, and it's a real privilege to reconnect these grief-stricken people with their children in spirit.

I remember being in the sanctuary at Arthur Findlay College on one of my yearly visits and the wonderful English tutor, Tony Stockwell, was welcoming all of us new students at the very beginning of the week. There were approximately one hundred of us seated in the large room, and I was sitting at the front. Tony asked for a show of hands to indicate how many of us present had experienced a personal tragedy that opened up our mediumistic gifts to us. I turned around to see approximately ninety people with hands in the air, and I found this to be utterly fascinating. As you will discover, each participant here has had a defining moment when they recognised the existence of their own mediumship abilities, yet all have had completely different experiences and sets of circumstances.

Chapter three

Paul Jacobs

I first met Paul at the college during my two-week stay in 2016. I wasn't in his class that year, but I did do a few exercises and tutorials with him, and I found Paul to be a wonderful tutor and an extremely gifted medium. In 2018, I was very grateful to be placed in Paul's group, and I feel that I learnt much from him that week. I was to do a five-day demonstrating course with Paul at the 'House of Spirit' in Hanover, Germany, in May 2020, but the Covid-19 pandemic put an end to all travel plans for everyone. My husband, Sergio, and I reconnected with both Paul and Biagio (Tropeano, the subject of a subsequent chapter) when they were in Melbourne in early 2020, where they were running a four-day mediumship workshop. Sergio and I both attended a charity platform demonstration at the Spiritualist church in Brunswick, and it was here that Sergio experienced his first mediumship reading of this type. It was most touching that Paul brought through Sergio's late mother and also our Sam. The evidence given was emotive, compelling and very accurate for both, and at that stage Paul had never met Sergio or had any previous mediumistic communication with Sam, which made the reading even more special.

Paul is an English medium and tutor at the Arthur Findlay College and has lived in Hanover, Germany, for the past fifteen years. He works extensively internationally. Paul's biography was published some years ago and is called *Paul, Man of Spirit*.

I had many experiences with the spirit world as a young boy, but I never knew what was really happening to me. My mother, Pauline, says that when I was very young I would come downstairs saying I had seen a man on the wall. These experiences were very real to me, and I now know they really happened.

Our family was of the Catholic faith, and I remember having a profound objective experience when I was thirteen or fourteen years of age. I was at church during the mass, kneeling down and looking at the altar. As I did this the priest disappeared and I saw myself standing in his place. This wasn't taking place in my mind; it was objectively happening as I watched on. Above the altar was a crucifix with Jesus on it, and he suddenly came alive, left the cross and came down to stand behind me. Jesus then 'walked' into my body and started speaking through me. I was watching all of this take place with my own eyes from where I was sitting in the pew. At the time I thought God was telling me to become a priest, but looking back now I know that it was the spirit world symbolising and telling me that one day I would speak with the voice of the spirits. I don't believe that Jesus really did this to me, but through symbolism from spirit the whole amazing experience was preparing me for what my future was to become. Through my own studies I have since learnt that symbology is a very important part of mediumship.

I grew up in the United Kingdom with my parents, Alfie and Pauline. I have one brother, Mark, and a sister, Leigh. Both are younger than me. Dad was a hard-working businessman who ran a market stall, and he had two clothing shops, selling mainly menswear. My mother originally worked in the clothing business too. Then she opened a hairdressing salon of her own, as she was an independent woman who wanted to earn and manage her own money. Tragically, I lost my father in a car accident when he was only forty years old. I was twenty, my brother was sixteen and my sister just fourteen. My mother was a very young widow, and it was an extremely difficult and trying time for everyone, as Dad was much loved and dearly missed.

My father's death took away my belief in God, and at that time I wanted nothing more to do with God or the Catholic faith, because I felt it had failed my family and me. I ended up taking over my father's business at the tender age of twenty. It was a massive undertaking, and thankfully everything went well for a while, but then I couldn't manage juggling everything and eventually I lost the lot. It was so heart-wrenching, and I was on the verge of having a nervous breakdown. I was drinking too much, and I was riddled with guilt because his business was the family asset my father left for me to manage.

After the failure of Dad's business I opened another small shop that sold hardware, ornaments and toys in the large, industrialised town of Dudley in West Midlands, not far from Birmingham. Again I lost everything, but it wasn't my fault this time; a new shopping centre had opened up out of the main town and my business was on a high street right next door to a busy supermarket, and a Marks and Spencer department store was very nearby. Both of these large businesses relocated to the new shopping centre precinct, and my little shop died a quick and natural death.

It was a very difficult period in my life, and I was out of work for a year, which was extremely hard to come to terms with. I returned home to live with my mother. I was fortunate to eventually find a suitable new job that I had experience in and felt comfortable with, so from the age of twenty-five to thirty-two I worked as a sales agent for a clothing company.

At the time I had recently moved into an old Victorian house in Wolverhampton, and once again I began having objective experiences with the spirit world, though I wasn't really aware of what was truly happening. At night-time while in bed I would hear my name being called, and I began seeing coloured lights and comets shooting across the room. There were also dark shapes standing beside my bed. In all honesty I thought the place was haunted. A few days later I was strolling down a road I had walked many times before and I saw a nondescript building with the light on; it was a church, and I just went in. I had no idea what to expect, and this was my first visit to a Spiritualist church.

As soon as I entered the church I was immediately struck that I had discovered something very special. I didn't know what it was, but I did understand that it was life changing in some unknown way. There was a church service taking place, and a medium was doing a demonstration; at the time I had no understanding that this is a key part of every Spiritualist church service. I didn't know what was happening, and the medium came to me with a contact from the spirit world. When she was halfway through the reading she said, 'I think I know you; you're Alfie's son.' The medium explained to the congregation that it wasn't fair to give me a contact publicly because she knew who I was, so she asked me if we could have a chat afterwards. The whole event was totally unexpected for me, and it turned out the medium was my great aunt on my father's side of the family. I only remotely knew of her, and she was called Aunt Lavinia.

It was six weeks after this chance meeting when Aunt Lavinia called me to ask if I was still going to the church. I said that I was, but I probably wouldn't continue doing so because to my way of thinking everything I was hearing from the mediums was a bit rubbishy. Not to be deterred, Aunt Lavinia said she was going to the Longton Spiritualist Church the following Sunday, and she invited me to go along with her. My great aunt went on to tell me this was Gordon Higginson's church, which meant nothing at all to me, as I didn't know who Gordon Higginson was. When we arrived, Gordon, who turned out to be the church president, was standing outside, and we shook hands; I then heard a voice in my head saying we were going to become friends. I didn't understand this at the time, but we did in fact become very good friends over the ensuing years.

At this point I should explain who Gordon Higginson was, as it has much relevance to my own pathway as a Spiritualist, medium and tutor. Gordon was known to be one of the finest mediums of our time. He was also a wonderful speaker and teacher of mediumship. Gordon was the longest-serving president of the Spiritualists National Union (SNU) from 1970 until his passing in 1993, and he was the principal of the Arthur Findlay College from 1979 until his death.

After my initial meeting with Gordon I started attending church services and seminars held in the church, but I certainly didn't believe for a minute that I was a medium myself. Unlike some attendees, I didn't go to church because I wanted to become a medium. I was there because I found the services to be extremely interesting and enlightening. Strangely, most weeks I would receive messages from the various mediums on the platform saying, 'One day you will stand here and you will be doing this.' I thought they were all crazy for saying such things. Regardless, at twenty-five years of age I decided to begin my own journey of discovery, without ever intending to become a medium at the end of it.

My first trip to Arthur Findlay College as a student was in 1984, and it came about because my great uncle invited me to go along with him. His wife, my great aunt Lavinia, had passed away by then, and though he was not a practising medium himself he liked to go to the college to do spiritual healing work. I didn't know if I was a medium or not; I was there simply because I wanted to learn more about the spirit world. Back then the college operated quite differently, and there wasn't group work in classes like they do now. It was mainly lectures, tutorials and mediumship demonstrations. That was how the students were taught; much of it was through observation rather than actual participation.

On the first evening of my course, Gordon Higginson was standing on the platform in front of the class, asking for a volunteer. No-one would stand up, me included, and Gordon said we were all a waste of time and asked why we were there. Gordon obviously knew my name, so he decided to call me out onto the platform as his 'volunteer'. There I innocently stood in front of seventy or eighty students, and Gordon said, 'Paul, I want you to make a contact with the spirit world.' I said I couldn't do that, as I'd never done it before. Gordon gave me no instruction at all; he said, 'Just ask who's there.' I somehow reached into the depths of my soul and cried out within, 'God, help me give this man what he wants.'

I then heard the word 'father', and I wasn't sure if this came from the spirit world or not, and to be honest I didn't care if I was wrong because I wasn't trying to prove if I was a medium or not. I announced to my fellow students that it was somebody's father, and with this Gordon said, 'Who does he want to speak to?' I innocently said that I didn't know. Gordon patiently replied, 'Ask, and allow the power to move you to where they want you to go'. One young woman in the audience stood out to me, so I went to her and asked if her father was in spirit. She answered, 'Yes'. It was quite nerve-wracking, and Gordon said, 'What do they want to say?' Again, I went into the depths of my own soul and silently cried for help. I then heard, 'I've only just passed and I've left her half a million pounds.' When I shared what I'd heard, the young woman replied, 'Yes, that's correct'. I was shocked, and students kept coming up and telling me that I was such a fantastic medium, and I kept saying, 'No, I'm not a medium!'

Gradually, I became very involved in driving Gordon all over the country to perform his mediumship demonstrations and in helping him to run the Longton Spiritualist Church. At the time my own position as a medium was still unknown to me, and I said to the spirit world that I would never believe I was a medium until Gordon told me I was.

At Gordon's suggestion I began attending development classes with a wonderful medium called Martin Young, and it was here that my mediumship strengthened for me and I gained clarity about my own capabilities. In 1986 I was invited by Gordon to become an organiser at the college, where my role was to book all of the mediums who were teaching each week throughout the year. I arranged the teaching program and took the bookings from the students for the paid one-on-one readings and spiritual assessments with the tutors.

One day I was having a cup of tea with Gordon, and he said to me he didn't understand why I wasn't taking my mediumship seriously and doing more with it. This came as a bit of a shock, but after that I decided to look at things differently and take on board what Gordon had said. By that stage I was thirty years old, and hearing these words made me realise that Gordon was acknowledging my mediumship capabilities. From then on I started to gain more and more experience with my readings, and after another two years I began doing my own mediumship demonstrations confidently in my own right at the churches and at the college, as a student.

At a tutorial given by Gordon he did a reading with me and said, 'You will be a long time starting your mediumship, but once you begin, you will go from strength to strength overnight.' This was very reassuring, but how this would take place was still a mystery to me. Becoming a full-time medium wasn't a conscious choice of mine; I was juggling so many things all at once, and it just turned out that way. I was busy accepting bookings at numerous churches to be the medium doing the platform demonstrations at the services, and I was also seeing people for private sittings after work. During these hectic years my primary source of income was still working full-time as a fashion sales agent. Something had to give, and I kept asking spirit if I should be working full-time as a medium or continue juggling both; frustratingly, I never received an answer.

Through Gordon I was invited to train as a tutor at the college in the late 1980s, and for this I am very grateful. Sadly, Gordon died in January 1993, and my first course teaching there as a qualified tutor was in March of that year. Over the years I had received a number of wonderful readings from Gordon, but now that he had passed I booked a reading with another medium who I greatly respected, Glyn Edwards, who is now also in the spirit world. Glyn said that spirit was saying it was my choice if I go full-time or not with my mediumship, but he added that there would always be enough work available to provide for my financial needs. The reading gave me the clarity and direction I needed, and I resigned from my sales agent position to work full-time as a medium.

The first couple of years were a struggle financially because most of my work was in churches, where you are lucky to receive five pounds, a cup of tea and a biscuit for your work on the platform. I was blessed that in my first week of going full-time I was invited to go abroad to work in Finland and then to teach for six weeks at

Arthur Findlay College. And after seven or eight years my career as a medium took off.

My life was on a path of self-destruction before finding my mediumship. I was acutely aware of this, and I asked God to help me. I can remember saying I would do anything at all to repay Him for getting my life back on track – nothing was out of bounds. I was prepared to clean the church, get involved in fundraising, anything at all to repay God for helping me. I didn't have to be a medium. The choice was mine to make, but I'm so grateful that I did become one. Mediumship and Spiritualism mean the world to me, and in many ways both have saved me. Looking back, I was so lucky to be introduced to some really fine mediums from the very beginning of my unfoldment, and I'm very aware that not everyone is so fortunate to have that happen to them.

My mediumship work has taken me to many countries, and I have lived in Hanover, Germany, for the past fifteen years. Prior to that I had been living and working in Amsterdam in The Netherlands. Through my work as a medium I met Biagio Tropeano in Italy at a seminar I was running; we became good friends, and Biagio needed help with some personal issues. Biagio, who is Italian born and raised, had already been living in Hanover for many years, and it was he who found the location of the House of Spirit, our own mediumship school in 2008. Biagio is also a medium and a well-known restaurateur and wine sommelier, so the name, House of Spirit, worked perfectly for us both to use. We ran many mediumship courses here over the years, welcoming students from all over the world. Sadly, the House of Spirit had to close in 2020, as the building was sold by our landlord.

Over the years I've taught mediumship in fifteen different countries including the United States, Canada, Australia, the United Kingdom, Germany, Switzerland, The Netherlands, Italy, Finland, Denmark and Sweden. I do a lot of the bookings myself, but also with the help of organisers at the other end; a lot of work is involved in the logistics of putting an event together. When I work with larger groups overseas I will often take Biagio with me, and we work together to give all the students the time and guidance they need, particularly with the platform demonstrating courses.

In the mid-nineties I worked quite a lot in the United States running various courses over a period of four or five years, and then I decided to stop because the students were too off the wall for me. The greater percentage of students were doing readings psychically and not working with their mediumship abilities, and as a result I stopped going. It was all about 'new age' and anything novel and different; at that time in the States you could even have a sitting with the aliens!

Spiritualism in America brought in all kinds of alternative ideas, and the majority of my students were looking for over-the-top stuff, and this wasn't for me. Thankfully, things have changed a lot and for the better in the United States; I've been going back there for the last five years, and I'm really enjoying the experience again. When I'm teaching I hate it when my students have previously been taught by other teachers to give the height, appearance and age of the spirit communicator, together with a whole 'checklist' of other anticipated things, rather than just letting the evidence flow naturally.

I feel Australia as a country is quite open in accepting mediumship; the people and culture there are not nearly as closed-minded as some other countries, like Germany and France. France is totally dismissive of mediumship, and you can't even publicly advertise mediumship demonstrations or private sittings; it all has to be done by word of mouth. Surprisingly to many, Italy is very open about mediumship, and much of the population regard mediums as extremely special people.

My original dream was to be a successful businessman and a millionaire, but now I'm just happy purely working for spirit, and this has been the total focus of my life. I have no time for any hobbies or other interests, and my working life is booked up for two and a half years in advance. Until recently I had always kept another home in England as a base, mainly because my mother is still living there, along with other members of my family, but I've now sold that property and bought a new home in Spain very near to Gibraltar. I love the beach and the sunshine, and I know that this will be perfect as I will eventually slow down in my mediumship teaching and travels. I live very much out of a suitcase, and home to me is wherever I am at the time. My mother says I should have been born with wheels, not feet!

My mother morally supports me very much in my work as a medium, and in so many other ways as well. Mum loves what I do, and she still attends my platform demonstrations when I'm in the United Kingdom, just so she can see me work. Years ago Mum was a volunteer for a long time at Arthur Findlay College on Open Week, and many of the curtains and drapes at the college were handmade by her. She is quite remarkable. Mum calls herself a Catholic still, but she doesn't go to church any longer. She hopes I'm wrong about the afterlife, because Mum says she's spent all of her life worrying about her children and she doesn't want to spend an eternity worrying about us as well!

My grandmother on Mum's side of the family was very mediumistic, but she was also a bit anti such things, because of her staunch Catholic beliefs. She thought it was okay to use her mediumship abilities for herself but not to make spirit contacts for other people. My grandmother was upset with me for becoming a spiritualist, and she asked me to become a Catholic priest instead. My own mother could have easily become a medium, but she was not at all interested, and I believe that mediumship abilities are in the genes of all families. Catholics used to believe that only God should make contact with the spirit world. The rules have thankfully been relaxed these days, and now you are allowed to have spirit contact with your own family personally, but not through using a medium.

In the mid-nineties I worked a lot in Italy, and I had many priests covertly come to me for readings, even though the church was very anti the practice. In the past I was associated with an organisation in Italy that was set up by a priest to help parents who had lost their children. I would do readings for these families to help them to heal in some way, and the priest completely understood the desperate need of these parents to reconnect with their children in spirit, and he facilitated this happening via me. The curiosity about mediumship is very much present with the priests, but sadly their religion doesn't agree with them embracing it openly or otherwise.

There is something in the Catholic religion and its rituals that creates a certain 'power', and I find this to be very close to what mediumship is all about. I once examined the religions of ten of the top male mediums I knew, and of them, eight were Catholics. Oddly, Gordon Higginson was not a Catholic. His mother used to do the cleaning and play the organ at a Christian church, where she often took Gordon along with her when he was a young boy. It was predicted by a medium when Gordon's mother was a young girl that she would have a son, and between them they would give one hundred years of service to the spirit world.

Most readings are not remembered by the medium because the information is not for us; it's for the recipient. I will never forget a reading I did when I was president of the Longton Church after Gordon Higginson passed. A woman came into the church after the service had already started, and I recognised her as someone who had been coming every week for about two years. She always came late and left early, never speaking to anyone, and she never received a contact from spirit either. I was walking down the aisle of the church, and something made me stop at this woman at the end of the pew. I asked her if she wanted me to arrange a private reading for her and she simply said, 'Please'.

It was arranged, and I did the sitting for her the next night. As I commenced the reading a young woman in spirit came forward, and I sensed immediately that this was the woman's daughter, who she verified had passed. Her daughter's ability to communicate with me was amazing, and it was not at all difficult to do the reading. Afterwards, the mother told me that when I asked her if she wanted a reading, she was ready to commit suicide, as she had been waiting for two years to hear from her daughter.

After two or three more sittings the woman asked me if I would see her husband as well, and I agreed. I was very aware that I would need to find some new information from their daughter in spirit, because so much good evidence had already been brought forward in the previous sittings. At the reading I knew the father wasn't buying a thing I was saying, and I felt that I had failed them both. There was no point in continuing, so I said I was going to bring the reading to a close. I told them I wanted to say some words that were being given from their daughter, which I also added wouldn't prove anything, as they were not actual evidence. I said, 'You're the best father in the world, and I wouldn't change you for anything.' With this, the man completely broke down, and I asked his wife what I had said wrong. She answered that the last time they saw their daughter they told her that her dad wasn't her biological father, and yet these were their daughter's words to him. Their daughter's message was the actual evidence of her survival into the spirit world, and nothing more was needed.

The same couple came again for one last reading, and the mother said how much I had helped them, but even after all of the evidence I had given there was one last thing that had never been shared. They wanted me to tell them their daughter's nickname. Requests such as this are always very difficult, as the spirit determines what is shared, not the medium. I began the reading, and I said, 'Your daughter had a favourite cartoon character, and there was a picture of this character in a frame, by the bed.' I could see this picture clearly, and they answered, 'Yes'. I said, 'It's, Betty Boop' and with that, the woman burst into tears. Betty Boop was who I saw in the picture, and it was also their daughter's nickname!

When it comes to my own death, I'm not afraid to die, though I am apprehensive about how I'll go. I am, however, looking forward to exploring the spirit world properly. I have experienced moments over the years when I have been taken into the spirit world to see it firsthand. This has helped so much with my own conviction about the reality of it. Spirit has allowed me to experience what happened to my father in the car accident and in his transition into the spirit world. I got to 'feel' what my dad felt on his death, and I could 'see' where he went afterwards, and it was all truly remarkable. This amazing experience has allowed me to know that the soul moves out of the body just prior to the physical body dying, and there is no pain in the actual entering of the spirit world.

Over the years I had to step back from many good friends when I first started my work as a medium, as they didn't understand what I was doing with my mediumship journey. Strangely, they are starting to re-enter my life now all these years on, and we have thankfully reconnected. We never really fell out; we were all just on different pathways in life. I remember they would say to me, 'Are you going to another one of those death and dying things?' Instead of me going with them to a nightclub! Thankfully, with years of acquired maturity my old mates are way more accepting of me and what I do now.

I have always wanted to remain very normal as a person, and I have never wanted to be put on a pedestal. At Arthur Findlay in my early days, I would be drinking at the bar and dancing with the students and people would comment how surprised they were by my behaviour, because I was a spiritual medium. I would say to them, 'I'm a human being!' We must keep the balance; we are living in a physical world, and we must be a part of this world on a day-to-day basis. We can't try to live constantly connected to the spirit world; we need to find a workable balance. It's important to understand that mediums are the same as everyone else; we just have a wonderful special ability.

I have seen many people attend Arthur Findlay who really want to do this work, but they don't have the right abilities to be an evidential medium. Rather than discouraging them, I find ways to utilise their spiritual side, as they may make a wonderful speaker at the church services. They will still be working for spirit, but in a different capacity to what the mediums contribute.

I feel that there are too many people out there with mediumship abilities who believe they must become full-time mediums or have a career change that isn't necessarily good for them. If things don't work out as planned, these people often tend to blame the spirit world if they aren't busy enough with their work, but it's important to understand that ultimately it was them who made the change, not spirit.

International medium and tutor
Age, 63
Hanover, Germany

www.mediumpauljacobs.com
paulmartinjacobs@icloud.com

Chapter four

BIAGIO TROPEANO

Biagio also gave a wonderful platform demonstration of mediumship at the same event in Melbourne that I mentioned previously. I found his energy to be engaging, trusting and compassionate; he's also very funny. Biagio and Paul came back to our home for drinks after the event, and for both of us it felt like we had known Biagio for years; he is someone who has that wonderful effect on you. Biagio's story is very different to that of many of the other mediums, as he still works professionally as a restaurateur and sommelier at Tropeano di-Vino in Hanover, Germany. Biagio also practises his mediumship and healing work on a part-time basis, which takes him internationally. Biagio is Italian born and has lived in Germany for over forty years.

It is my opinion that everyone can do mediumship in one way or another. Some people can make contact with the spirit world and read for complete strangers, while others can communicate knowingly with their own loved ones, but much more so on a private and personal level. Like many mediums, the story of my own mediumship unfoldment is neither straightforward nor predictable, and I would like to share it with you here.

I am Italian and was born in Bari, Puglia, in the southern part of Italy. I moved with my family to Milan in northern Italy when I was very young, still a baby of one or two years in age. My parents relocated to the north for a change of life and to find work, as things were very harsh financially, particularly in the southern part of the country. There are five children in my family; I have an older brother, then myself and there are three younger sisters.

Growing up, I didn't have any personal involvement with mediumship or the spirit world, but I did have a great aunt on my father's side of the family who was a Tarot card reader in Puglia. As the story goes, everyone knew of my great aunt Teresa and her amazing psychic and mediumship abilities. She was well respected in her community and highly regarded for being very accurate with her Tarot card readings. This very remarkable woman was my father's aunt, and when he was a little boy his own mother knew she was dying, so, knowing this, her sister took my father and the other seven children in and raised them all by herself. My great aunt had never married, so she was childless, and this was an incredible act of kindness on her part. This wonderful woman also raised one of her niece's children, as she had ten children of her own and needed help to care for them all. By that stage my father's aunt was very old, but she still took in another child.

When I was a young boy we would visit my great aunt in Puglia, where she lived. No-one was allowed to enter her bedroom, but of course we would sneak in anyway only to be shocked by what was in there. Human bones had been collected from the cemetery, and she had shrunken heads and other unexplainable things. It was all very strange and probably totally forbidden by the Church and quite possibly by the law as well. These macabre treasures were supposedly hidden from us children, but we always found them and we liked the mystery of them; however, we had no concept of their true purpose, which included practising witchcraft. On my mother's side of the family there was an aunt who could look accurately into the future, and to me as a seven-year-old this was also amazing.

I'm not sure if I was influenced in some way by these old relatives, but when I was thirteen or fourteen years old my sisters and I would play games reading Tarot cards for one another. We were discovered by our parents and told that 'as good Christians, we shouldn't play with Tarot cards', so we all stopped immediately. I was a very religious child and an altar boy from the ages of six till twelve in the Catholic Church. I regularly attended two masses every Sunday, one in the morning and the evening prayer. I found my Catholic religion to be a very intensive experience.

Work has always been of great importance in my family and an absolute necessity. My father did many different types of jobs during his lifetime, anything at all to earn money to support us. Predominately he worked in a foundry and forged metalwork. Papa toiled there for many years, and the work was hard, the hours were long and it was not particularly safe. As a result my father got bone cancer caused by lead poisoning from all of the exposure to handling the toxic metals over many years. Even with his serious illness, he lived until he was seventy-nine years old and sadly passed in 2016.

Like all Italian women of that time, my mother stayed at home to raise the family, and she didn't work outside of the home when we were young. It wasn't a matter of choice; married women had to stay at home, and it was expected of them. Before getting married my mother was a very talented seamstress, and she would make the most beautiful clothes and other exceptional items. My mother had a wonderful reputation as a skilled sewer, and she always loved creating beautiful things.

As an eight-year-old, every day after school I worked at a little bar where I would carry the empty bottles downstairs into the cellar to help the owner's wife. I was paid 5,000 lire a week for my work, which was an amazing amount of money to me, and it allowed to me buy an ice cream and have enough left over to go to the cinema. I was fascinated by the running of the bar, and soon I started to learn how to make coffee for the customers.

Though happy at the bar, when I was aged ten another small business owner approached me and offered me 10,000 lire per week to work at his flower shop, delivering flowers on my bicycle. I was also expected to deliver huge house plants, which were often bigger than me, yet somehow I got them onto the rack on my bike and to their destination safely. It was here that I also learnt about floristry and how to make beautiful floral arrangements.

I was a very good student, and when my parents asked what I wanted to do after I finished high school I innocently said I wanted to become a doctor or a lawyer. When I made my grand announcement my parents said, 'From what?', meaning that we didn't have the finances to allow me to study at university and certainly not for the number of years required to complete a medical or law degree. I was fourteen years old, and my mother suggested as a strange compromise that I go to Amerigo Vespucci in Milan and study hospitality. The school offered many different courses; I could train to become a chef, waiter, a hotel receptionist or I could seek a career in hotel management.

My mother didn't want me to do the hotel reception training, as she thought my role would be to just hand out the room keys, and I saw the sense in what she was saying. I took the option of training as a waiter because it offered me the opportunity to learn another language, either English or German, and I knew this would be beneficial to me. I started my studies at the hospitality school and at the same time – through my hospitality teacher, Gino Marcialis, who was a very famous barman in Italy in the 1960s and 1970s – I became a junior waiter and dishwasher at Piccolo Gourmet. I was very fortunate that Gino knew the sommelier and owner of Piccolo Gourmet, Giuseppe Birolini, who later became my mentor and taught me all about wine.

It was a very difficult time. I was constantly exhausted by working at the restaurant at night and attending school during the day. My father didn't seem to understand where I was every night, and he wrongly assumed that I was out partying, even though he had been told what I was doing, so he wasn't at all supportive of what I was going through.

I chose to study German as my preferred language, and my plan was to live and work in Germany while learning how to speak the language. My parents didn't seem to understand how important this was to me, and they offered no real support in helping me to achieve what I had worked so hard to accomplish in my four years at the hospitality school. I received a letter from the five-star Park Hotel in Bremen, Germany, offering me a waitering position in their restaurant, and I was to start work the following year. I was quietly jubilant.

My dream was being realised, and I was soon to be on my way to Germany, yet my father still didn't understand that I had finally achieved what I had strived so hard for. He wouldn't speak to me at all, and I know now that he was afraid of losing me as a child and this was his way of dealing with his emotions. Regardless, I reluctantly left my family and settled in well at the restaurant in Bremen to begin my hospitality work and my language studies.

In 1982, I met my German-born wife and we married and stayed living in Bremen. A wonderful opportunity arose in 1983, and I was offered a brand-new position of sommelier at the Park Hotel. I became the first sommelier in Germany. My family grew, and our first daughter, Sarah, was born in 1983, and Christina followed in 1986. We later moved from Bremen to Hanover, and in 1997 I opened my first restaurant, called Tropeano, and it was very successful. My parents came from Milan for the opening, and when my father saw our family name on the awning, I could see how proud and happy he was for me at last. Wine and beverages became my prime focus, and in 1995 I was awarded the title of Sommelier of the Year for all of Germany, something I am honoured to have received.

When I started working at the restaurant in Bremen in the early 1980s, I began to unintentionally tap into my undiscovered psychic abilities. While working at the restaurant I started offering a complementary glass of grappa to the diners after dinner, and through using my own psychic understanding I would intuitively always choose the right type of grappa to be of liking to each guest. The customers were amazed that I could select the best-tasting grappa from around sixty different varieties, and I always chose one that suited their tastebuds perfectly. The local newspaper ran a story about me, and they called me the 'Grappa Oracle', because of my ability to instinctively know what people liked.

After giving the diners their complementary night cap, I would then give them a brief psychic reading at the table, telling them a lot of information about themselves. I really had no idea what I was doing. I just intuitively knew certain things about these complete strangers. The accuracy of the readings were incredible, and this astounded not only them but me too. I now know and understand why my own mediumship development happened so very quickly later on – because I had already been unknowingly doing different types of readings for many years.

In 2001, when I was forty, I felt that my wife and two daughters didn't really need me anymore; the girls were at school, and my wife and I had drifted apart. I knew there was something missing in my life, and I felt I was verging on some type of depression. I felt that if I wasn't there tomorrow then nobody would really care, and I knew this was a very bad way to be thinking. After six months of feeling like this, I finally went to see a doctor; he was very worried about me and the state of my overall health, so I was hospitalised immediately. I was also suffering from an undiagnosed infection, and I couldn't breathe properly as my lungs were totally full of fluid.

That night I saw someone in my hospital room, and they were sitting on my bed. I asked the nurse in the morning who had visited me during the night, and she said that no-one else had been in my room. While I saw someone in my room, I could also smell the perfume of fresh flowers very clearly. The next day an aunt called me at the hospital from Italy and said she had been praying for me to Saint Padre Pio. Folklore has it that whenever this saint is around he leaves the scent of flowers, and this gave me hope that I would get better.

My parents came from Italy to see me, and everyone was extremely worried about my health. My mental state was still not good either, but when I saw how much I was loved and supported by my family, after two days I started to miraculously feel well again. I was very aware of the power of the mind, and I knew that something very special was taking place within me. My doctor was shocked that I recovered so quickly, and I was soon able to return home.

I told my wife about what my aunt had said about Saint Padre Pio, and she tried to find a documentary tape at the video store that would tell me more about this fascinating man. She looked everywhere and at many different video shops but still had no luck. Not long afterwards I was looking in my briefcase, and I found an envelope with a video tape inside. I opened it, and there was the story of Saint Padre Pio. To this day I have no idea where the tape came from, but I was meant to watch his story so I could finally appreciate that there was more to life than meets the eye. The spiritual side of me was at last awakened, and my life took a completely different turn from then on.

After this experience I started looking for answers, and after much research I began following a spiritual guru from India called Baba Bedi. From him I learnt that when the lungs are affected with sickness, as mine were, the sufferer has many unexpressed emotions to deal with. This was a very different way for me to think and act; it was all quite instinctive, but I knew I was on the right track by doing things that weren't mainstream. I was open to all sorts of new ideas and experiences, and somewhere I read that an English medium called Paul Jacobs was going to be in Pesaro in Italy, running a seminar about mediumship. I knew nothing at all about mediumship, but I also knew I needed to attend Paul's workshop.

In 2003 I travelled to Italy to attend the mediumship seminar with Paul, and he and I immediately became very good friends. At the workshop I discovered I had a natural ability to connect with the spirit world. It had always been there; I just wasn't aware of it. At the same time as I was exploring my own mediumship abilities, I was also in the process of opening my second restaurant in Hanover called Tropeano Di-Vino. When I returned to Germany from Italy I worked to complete the restaurant, and it opened later in 2003. I had made lots of wonderful new friends in Pesaro, and many of these people travelled to Germany to celebrate my new business venture at the opening, including Paul.

Prior to meeting Paul, I was a real 'man of the church', and I was happy to be told how to think, but through Paul and Spiritualism I learnt how to think more for myself. In many ways I became more connected to God than I had ever been before. Now I also understand the power of healing, which is my first love in my spiritual work. I believe that religions of all kinds are the poison of humanity because God has been forgotten along the way and so many wars and atrocities have been committed over the centuries in the name of God. To me, this is very wrong.

Through working with Paul as my mentor and teacher my mediumship started to flourish, and I attended another seminar being run by him at the Arthur Findlay College in the United Kingdom. After my wonderful experience at the college I went with Paul to Lugano in Switzerland to help him at a three-day workshop he was running there. Paul wanted me to gain some firsthand experience in private mediumship sittings, so he arranged for me to do eight thirty-minute sittings a day over three days with his students. I had never formally read for anyone prior to this, but Paul believed in me and my capabilities, so I trusted in him completely. The readings all went very well, and I loved doing them.

I had seen Paul do mediumship demonstrations many times before, but this was all still very new to me, and on the first night Paul got me up to do platform demonstrations with him in front of two hundred and fifty people! I honestly thought I was going to die; I was terrified, and I did the readings in my native Italian, as many Swiss people understand the language, and it all went perfectly. It was very funny afterwards because all of these people were gathering around and speaking to me in Italian, and Paul came out and said, 'Hey, I'm the star here!' It was a wonderful beginning for me, and Paul was amazing in how he taught me to trust in myself and to believe in what I can do.

Paul kept on pushing me to become a full-time working medium, but I still wanted to run my restaurant. I explained to Paul that in many ways I was still working in a very spiritual way in the restaurant, because people would come to me all the time to share their sad stories and ask my advice. I cannot tell you how many relationships I have saved just by allowing people to share their grief and problems with me. I always want to make people feel good and well cared for, and I know I can and do lift the spirits of the people who come into the restaurant. For me that is just as important as being able to serve them great food and beautiful wine.

I have since returned a few times to the Arthur Findlay College as a guest tutor, where I have worked helping Paul on his mediumship courses. I love doing this, and I teach my own groups of students in accordance with what I have been taught by Paul. I have also been involved in a joint venture with Paul at the House of Spirit in Hanover, which is a small teaching school for mediums, but we closed unfortunately in 2020 because our premises was sold by the owner.

In Germany mediumship is not widely understood, and sadly this is due to there being so many charlatans in existence, who have been publicly ridiculed and exposed over the years. Both Paul and I have been fighting against these unscrupulous people for a long time because these con artists give mediumship a bad name and this makes it very difficult for the genuine mediums. A lot of people in Hanover have no idea that I am a medium; I don't say anything because I know that most won't understand at all and many may think I have been drinking too much of the wine I serve! Our closest friends are aware that I am both a restaurateur, sommelier and a medium, and they know and accept what Paul does with his work, as he is widely known internationally as a tutor and medium.

Mediumship programs on TV generally make a mockery of mediumship as a practice, and of the mediums. For me mediums should always be portrayed as normal people who have a wonderful ability to communicate naturally with the spirit world, and it should always be done without any theatrics or silly fanfare.

About two years after starting my mediumship unfoldment I went back to Italy to attend a wine fair in Verona and then to visit my parents in Milan. My mother said she had an interesting dream in which she saw me working publicly in front of at least two hundred people on a platform, and I was giving some sort of healing to the people. I was totally shocked by her words, and then she said that the palms of my hands were very red in colour. When I do my healing work my hands do become a vivid red, just like my mother saw in her dream.

The amazing thing about my mother's dream is that neither of my parents knew I was a medium and healer, and they also had no idea about what Paul did professionally. On another occasion, while Paul was with me at my parents' home, my mother suddenly gave Paul a dress ring to hold and she asked him to tell her about the original owner of the ring. This practice is called psychometry, and I have no idea how my mother could have known that Paul could do a reading from holding a possession of someone in spirit, but she did!

My mother has been relentless; another time Paul and I were at the supermarket in Milan, and she rang my mobile phone and insisted on speaking to Paul. I kept saying to her, 'You don't speak English and Paul doesn't speak Italian!' Eventually, my mother calmed down enough to tell me that her friend had just died and she wanted to speak to her through Paul. She instinctively knew Paul could communicate with the dead, even though she had never been told this by either of us. When we got back to the house Paul did a reading for my mother, and he was able to communicate with her friend, who offered evidence of her survival into the spirit world. This was both amazing and comforting to my mother.

One of my sisters has had a reading with Paul, and she believes fully in what we both do, which is reassuring to me. My two adult daughters, Sarah and Christina, don't ever talk to me about my mediumship work; they have seen me working at numerous platform demonstrations, and to them it's just Dad doing his mediumship work and nothing more is ever discussed about it. What I do is so normal and acceptable to them, and there is no mystery in it at all.

One year on my parents' yearly visit to Germany, my father wanted to know if I had any Italian cards so we could play a traditional card game. I said I didn't have any of the special cards we needed to play our particular game. The following year on their annual visit my father brought with him a deck of Italian cards that had once belonged to his aunt Teresa, who was the amazing medium I mentioned earlier. To my father they were just normal Italian playing cards, and he wanted me to keep them so we would have a pack to play cards with on his visits.

Aunt Teresa used these normal Italian cards to do her Tarot readings with, and I remember when I was young my great aunt wanted to know how she would be able to choose who to pass her special mediumship abilities on to. I presume she was wondering which one of us children had potential to develop as a medium. Aunt Teresa never made that choice when she lived, but now all these decades later, my father had innocently brought her special Tarot cards to me. The cards and her wonderful mediumship abilities are now mine.

My mediumship work and teaching has allowed me to travel extensively, and I have travelled with Paul to run yearly seminars in Australia. I have worked in Germany (at the House of Spirit), Switzerland, the United Kingdom, The Netherlands, Italy and the United States. In Hanover I do private sittings and healing sessions with my clients, and I love doing these. It's interesting because when I'm busy with the restaurant no-one ever books a reading with me, but as soon as I have a quiet time in my hospitality business my mediumship bookings resume again. It's like the spirit world is only sending me clients when I have time to see them.

It is my understanding that the spirit world wanted me to do this type of work, which is why my mediumship unfoldment happened very naturally and extremely quickly. My mediumship has changed my life in so many positive ways. I find that it grounds me, and I regard both my restaurant and my mediumship as the two aspects of my life that fully express who I am in this world and why I am here. Selfishness, ego and arrogance must be removed from the person if they want to develop, as these traits cannot exist on any level when working with mediumship.

My life is very busy and extremely rewarding. I still have my restaurant, Tropeano Di- Vino, and when I'm not overseas, I work seven days a week and I wouldn't have it any other way.

Restaurateur, sommelier, teacher, healer and medium
Age, 60
Hanover, Germany

www.restaurant-tropeano.de
biagiotropeano@gmail.com

Chapter five

PAMELA POLLINGTON

I first met Pamela at the Arthur Findlay College a couple of years ago when we were both put into the same class. As students, we tend not to talk about ourselves or our personal circumstances at all, as we don't want to share any information that may come up in the many readings we do in the classes. However, I did discover through watching the platform demonstration sessions that Pamela had also lost a child. We spoke later, and I discovered that her daughter, Charlene, and our son, Sam, had passed only months apart in 2012. I'm so grateful that Pamela was prepared to share the heartbreak of Charlene's tragic death and her own unconventional experiences as a young woman in the grip of the Jehovah's Witnesses church. Pamela works with her husband in their family newsagency business and is a practising medium in the United Kingdom.

I always liked to think of myself as a normal little girl when I was growing up, but looking back it wasn't really the case. My older sister, Angela, and I were born in Hersham, Surrey, in the United Kingdom to our parents, Marilyn and Fred. My father was a maintenance foreman at the local greyhound kennels, and my mother was a caregiver in an aged care home, where she worked the night shift. When I was six years old Mum walked out on my dad, and my parents divorced soon after. I then moved with my mother to live in the nearby town of Walton-on-Thames.

I was never allowed to have a voice around my father; in his eyes little girls were seen and not heard. My father was a man who instilled fear in me, as he had a quick temper and shouted a lot. Dad went on to remarry a woman who already had a son of her own, and together she and Dad had another baby boy.

I was christened in the local Church of England chapel; however, I attended Sunday school at the Baptist church in Walton-on-Thames. My mother was not really religious, but she did believe in Spiritualism and life after death. She had lost her own mother at twenty-four years of age, and her Spiritualist beliefs helped her to cope with her grief. I always had a spiritual thirst within me that I can't explain, and I would sometimes have weird premonitions and dreams without knowing what any of it meant.

When I was six years old I dreamt about a man who wore strange-looking square-rimmed green glasses. He had a black beard and wore a hat. In my dream he came up very close and looked directly into my face. Strangely, I wasn't frightened. The next morning when I got up I found an actual pair of the exact green glasses that the man was wearing in my dream. This was my first inkling that another kind of unseen world existed that was different to the one I lived in. I had no concept or understanding about the spirit world at all, but I also knew that this man wasn't an intruder in the house and he wasn't a real living person either.

At fourteen I met my future husband, David. Initially, I was attracted to the family environment around David; it seemed so normal by comparison to my own upbringing. On reflection I just really craved a normal family life like I saw other children enjoying. I was a 'latchkey' child who was left very much to my own devices, as Mum worked full-time to support us both. Though I soon came to realise that David's family was not as perfect as they looked from the outside. Regardless, it didn't take long for me to become quite immersed in all that David and his family were doing, and I became an extension to the family in lots of ways.

I was included in many of their daily activities, including personal situations. I remember that David's grandfather was dying, and the family, including myself, were to go and visit him. The night before we went I dreamt that the grandfather's bed had been moved downstairs into some sort of living area, and as soon as we arrived to see him, he would die. I found this dream to be very distressing, and I didn't dare tell anyone in their family, or mine, about it. As planned, I went with David, and his mother, Agnes, to visit her father the next day. This was the first time I had been to the grandfather's home, and when we arrived I was stunned to see him downstairs in his bed, which was in the lounge room. As we approached him to say hello, he recognised his daughter and suddenly took a turn and died – exactly like in my dream.

Agnes was a devoted follower in the Jehovah's Witnesses faith, and she was always on the look-out for future followers. Agnes was extremely strong willed, and it didn't take long before I was being drawn into learning all about this intriguing religious group. I was still only fourteen years old when I started studying with the Jehovah's Witnesses under the direction of Agnes, and just as she had intended, she had found another unwitting devotee. David and his father were both anti the Jehovah's Witnesses, and neither liked the Church's thinking or practices. I became Agnes's new best friend; she had wanted a new recruit, and she had found one in the young and naive girl I was back then. Together we would secretly study the Bible behind David's back, and my own mother had no idea how entrenched I had become in my Jehovah's Witnesses beliefs.

Around the same time my mother and sister were going to have a mediumship reading, and I was very curious to join them. I stupidly told David about it, and he wouldn't allow me to go. He said it was evil and wrong to have readings with mediums, and though I'd never seen one myself his opinion didn't feel right to me.

David and I married when I was eighteen, and not long afterwards we had two beautiful daughters. Charlene was born when I was twenty, and then Danielle arrived when I was twenty-two. When I was four months pregnant with Danielle, David walked out on us; we had been married four years by this stage, and I was now on my own with a baby and another one on the way. My experiences with male relationships often seemed to be very negative and always involved men inflicting abuse and control over a woman. My father treated both me and my mother in this way, and, sadly, I later also fell into accepting this pattern of abusive behaviour with David. I had a very misunderstood perception that all males acted this way, and it was somehow 'normal'.

During our marriage David was both physically and mentally abusive towards me, and he was also unfaithful on many occasions. My mother-in-law, Agnes, was still totally controlling, and I continued to study the Bible on and off with her. After we separated and with David out of the way, Agnes insisted I could now officially join the Jehovah's Witnesses and attend the Kingdom Hall meetings with her. David somehow heard through someone that the girls and I were at Kingdom Hall with his mother, and word got to us during the service that David was waiting outside and he wanted to see his young daughters.

The ever-controlling Agnes told me not to go out and see David; she insisted that he must agree to study with the Jehovah's Witnesses for six months, and if he kept his promise to do this then I could consider taking him back. This was all too much for me, and I stopped attending the Jehovah's Witnesses services altogether. I had no life of my own, and I felt like a puppet on a string. My mother-in-law had controlled much of my life, then my husband and now this fanatical religion as well. I knew that by not attending the religious services I could finally distance myself from Agnes and start to rebuild my life in my own way.

When Danielle was nine months old and Charlene was three I reconnected with Guy, a lovely old schoolfriend who I had met as a twelve-year-old. We were good friends at school, and Guy and I had no secrets; he knew about my past with the Jehovah's Witnesses religion, and by that stage I had left the Church, David and Agnes well behind me. Guy and I got married when we were both twenty-five and settled down happily with both of the girls.

Not that long after our wedding, Agnes turned up unannounced at our house, and she was holding a copy of the Jehovah's Witnesses *Watchtower* magazine. She stood at our front door and told me if I didn't resume with the Jehovah's Witnesses, I would have the blood of my children on my hands. I honestly felt that my girls would die if I didn't rejoin, so once again I was drawn back into the clutches of both Agnes and the Church; I started studying again and attending services at the Kingdom Hall.

Thankfully, Guy was very patient and understanding about respecting whatever made me happy, and he supported my desire to go back to the Jehovah's Witnesses faith, even though he had no interest in it himself. The Jehovah's Witnesses are self-portrayed as a fair religion, but I know now that what they practice is straight-out brainwashing and scare-mongering based on human frailty and fear. Agnes was happy to enforce their scare tactics. When I was pregnant with Melissa, my third child, I was persuaded by Agnes to get baptised into the Jehovah's Witnesses faith, which I did. I later had another daughter, called Rebekah, who was born in 1997, and for the next twelve years I would take all four girls along with me to the Kingdom Hall.

Guy's family hated my involvement with the Jehovah's Witnesses Church, which was more like a cult in their eyes, and this really put a strain on family relationships, particularly at Christmas time. The

Jehovah's Witnesses don't celebrate Christmas; so we couldn't either! The religion really messed with my brain. Agnes was relentless, and she even tried to make me promote the Church to Guy and his family. She was shameless in her heavy-handed approach, and it took me another five years to finally and permanently leave the Church. The final blow came when I discovered that one of my daughters was being sexually groomed by a member of the church at the Kingdom Hall. I was totally disgusted, and after leaving the Jehovah's Witnesses I never wanted to be a part of any religion ever again.

On the morning of the accident I intuitively knew something was going to happen to Charlene; she was rushing about madly, running late for school, and she hurried out the door without saying goodbye and jumped on her bike. It was only ten minutes later when I heard an emergency vehicle siren, and I instinctively knew that the ambulance was for her. The phone rang and the caller asked me to go to the accident site, which wasn't very far from our home.

Apparently, the skip lorry was turning left on a green light and Charlene tried to pass it on the left-hand side, presumably unaware that it was turning. Charlene was hit by the lorry and run over. Meanwhile, a police car just happened to be passing in the opposite direction going to another incident, and this meant that Charlene had immediate police attention and an ambulance was called straight away.

The front wheels of the lorry clipped Charlene's bike and brought her and the bike down and the back wheels of the lorry went over her body. She was so lucky because the bike frame lay over her torso in the exact position that protected her major organs from being crushed. However, her pelvis was badly broken, she had a fractured neck vertebrae and severe trauma to the head.

A second ambulance was called for because of Charlene's shocking injuries, and she had to be resuscitated three times in the ambulance on the way to the hospital. The ambulance personnel were made aware I was still a member of the Jehovah's Witnesses at the time, and as a result a court order was drawn up immediately and put in place so Charlene would receive all the medical attention needed, even if it went against the beliefs of the Church. A blood transfusion was required because of Charlene's terrible injuries; however, the Jehovah's Witnesses Church doesn't allow such procedures. Thankfully, we had the court order, and David, Charlene's father, gave the hospital permission to do whatever was needed to save her life.

After six weeks in hospital in a combination of intensive care and the children's ward, Charlene was finally allowed to come home, and she spent a very long time moving about in a wheelchair. Her injuries were extensive and very slow to mend, but eventually her pelvis healed, leaving her with a dropped foot because of the nerve damage that had affected her leg. Life became very difficult for Charlene after the accident. She used to dance and play sport, and now she could no longer participate, and understandably this affected her confidence and changed her personality considerably.

At fifteen, Charlene had to have more surgery to try to fix the mobility in her foot, but tragically the operation didn't work. Consequently, Charlene became even more depressed, as she would never gain full mobility of her foot, and this affected her movement. Charlene was awarded 65,000 pounds in compensation for the accident, which she could access once she turned eighteen.

Charlene was not following our family house rules, and she was difficult to control, so at eighteen she decided to move out of our home and get a flat with her boyfriend, Owen. By law, Charlene was of age and able access her compensation money, so there wasn't anything we could do to prevent this. Owen and Charlene were not a good influence on one another; they were constantly arguing, and again we were powerless to step in.

Charlene's life was spiralling out of control. She started smoking dope and not taking care of herself, and Owen was an abusive heavy drinker. After yet another fight, Charlene took an overdose of sleeping tablets; she thankfully survived, and her doctor put her on antidepressants to cope with her mental health. Owen and Charlene separated, and then she discovered she was pregnant with her son, Toby. Charlene was nineteen years of age at the time.

Toby was born in 2008. He was later diagnosed as autistic and, of course, Charlene wrongly blamed herself for this. Owen reappeared, and the two of them ended up getting back together, but once again the relationship didn't work out and Charlene took another overdose of sleeping tablets and was admitted to a high-dependency hospital ward where she nearly died. A suicide note was left by Charlene asking me to keep Toby, as she felt that everything she touched turned to crap. Charlene had no self-confidence at all, and she always blamed herself for everything that went wrong. Guy and I decided we were going to take care of Toby, but once Charlene was discharged from hospital she changed her mind and wanted Toby back living with her.

In 2011 Charlene met Daniel, and they started dating. We really didn't want to meet Daniel because I'd heard he was not a good lad, and I just knew it wouldn't end well. Charlene was furious with me for not wanting to meet Daniel, but we agreed to meet if they were still together after three months. I invited Charlene and Daniel over on Boxing Day for dinner so we could finally meet him and hopefully make peace. The evening went very well for everyone, and at last a truce was made between Charlene and me.

It didn't take long – as I had always feared, things weren't at all good between Charlene and Daniel. A neighbour of theirs told me that a lot of arguing happened regularly between them both, and on New Year's Eve, just a few days after our Boxing Day dinner, another argument erupted and Charlene was seen by the neighbour hiding from Daniel outside their flat.

Charlene had bought Daniel tickets to a football match for his Christmas present, and they were both to watch the game together on 8 January 2012. It was Danielle's twenty-first birthday dinner on the same night as the football match, and we had Toby with us. It was getting late when we got home, and there was still no word from Charlene. We noticed that a note had been put through our front door; it was from Daniel's aunt saying there had been an accident. Without knowing any more, I knew instinctively that Charlene was dead.

Premonitions have always been very real for me, and quite often they have been extremely accurate and therefore disturbing. I always intuitively knew that I would lose one of my four daughters, and this frightened me so much, and I had recently experienced a vision of me burying one of my girls. Two weeks later, Charlene died. Charlene had always said to me she knew she would die young and her death would be a traumatic one. It seems now she was very intuitive about her own tragic future.

On social media it was reported that a girl had been killed at Wimbledon Station, so I called the police, and this was verified, but nothing more was said about who it was or what had happened. I gave a description of Charlene and who she was with, and I was told that a police car was being sent to our home. The police had access to the train station's CCTV, which showed Charlene and Daniel arguing, and Charlene was then seen sitting on the edge of the train platform. Her mobile phone had been thrown onto the tracks, and Daniel was seen going off to find a staff member to help them to retrieve the phone.

After he left, Charlene went to another platform and climbed down to get away from Daniel. She was seen on CCTV hiding under the lip of the station platform, obviously hoping not to be seen by him. The footage then showed that for five minutes Charlene tried desperately to clamber back up onto the platform, but due to the nerve damage in her leg and foot, she couldn't get enough leverage to climb back up to safety. A few seconds before she died, a station cleaner had noticed Charlene and dropped his equipment and raced to help her up. It was too late; Charlene fell backwards just as the train came into the station. Her death was instant. It was not suicide, but she had inadvertently and tragically put herself in this dangerous and deadly situation. Charlene was only twenty-three when she died.

Our family was devastated by Charlene's death, and the horrible circumstances of how it happened, and nothing can prepare you for such a tragedy. I wasn't at all ready for what took place next either. My sister, Angela, had travelled to be with us after Charlene's accident and while staying she went to visit an old friend. There was another woman at her friend's home, who happened to be a medium, and this woman said to Angela, 'I need to see your sister.' A couple of days later this medium came to our house unannounced.

I had never had a mediumship reading before, and I really didn't know what to expect. We both went upstairs to what is now my own reading room. A connection was made immediately with Charlene's spirit, and the medium told me that Charlene had an issue with moving her toes properly and that she was madly looking to find her handbag. Charlene certainly had disabilities with her foot and her handbag was never found after the accident, so all of this evidence made perfect sense to me. The medium said Charlene was with someone else in spirit called David, and she could see a burnt-out car. David was Guy's cousin, and the medium said David took his own life in an intentional car accident that decapitated him and in which his car caught fire. All of this was totally true and absolutely accurate; I was amazed.

I found the mediumship reading to be very calming, and it made me feel so at peace. The medium asked me to go to Charlene's flat, where she said I would find a blue picture frame with a photograph in it, but she didn't say what the photo was of. What she said next astounded me; she said that Charlene wanted me to hang the blue-framed picture on the spare picture hook in the front room downstairs. There was a spare picture hook in our lounge room, but the medium had not been into that room, and she couldn't possibly have known this. After the reading I went to Charlene's flat, and after much looking eventually I found the blue-framed photo in question underneath a pile of paperwork. It was a beautiful photograph of Charlene and Toby!

I started going to the local Spiritualist church for the first time in my life, and I didn't know that Spiritualism was an actual recognised religion; I thought it was just somewhere you went to receive messages from your loved ones in spirit. At the same time Danielle began to see Charlene in spirit, and this really frightened her. The church ran a spiritual development group, and I thought this would help Danielle understand what she was experiencing in seeing Charlene's spirit around her. I decided to stay with her in the classes and to participate myself, but I really had no idea what to expect either.

It was never my intention to attend the circle group for my own mediumistic development; it was simply to be with Danielle to support her as she started to explore and develop her own mediumship abilities. Danielle found the circle confronting, and she was frightened of the spirit world, so she chose to not to pursue mediumship any further. It's apparent to me now that using any mediumship abilities is a choice, and not everyone is meant to utilise them during their lifetime. I had an alternative experience to Danielle; I loved all that I was taught, and I was able to do all of the exercises with relative ease.

I started to become a real 'workshop junkie', and I began going to as many mediumship workshops as possible; I loved everything about them. I was drawn to looking at the Arthur Findlay College. I had heard about it, and I started to seriously look at the courses they offered only a few months after Charlene's death. After my original mediumship reading after Charlene's accident, I decided to contact another medium, Andrew Manship, who had been recommended to me. He came to our house and did a wonderful reading for me. He also said I would be going to Arthur Findlay one day as a student. Andrew advised me to go on a course with a medium called Simon James. I hadn't said a word to Andrew about the college or about my curiosity in wanting to go there, so to me this was a very positive sign that felt just right.

I looked at the college's website and saw that this recommended medium, Simon James, was running a course in March 2013. I phoned the college sometime late in 2012, and I was told that the course was already fully booked, so I agreed to be waitlisted. I was initially very disappointed at missing out, but two weeks before the start date in March I received a phone call saying there was a late cancellation and a single room was available, just as I had hoped for.

My experience at the college was a life-changing one, and my mediumship abilities were confirmed by the tutors. Though a late starter, I have since attended another ten weeks at the college, and I've completed further mediumship training at Hampton Hill Spiritualist Church in Hampton and various mediumship courses at the Barbanell Centre in Stafford. I'm now a qualified healer after fulfilling all of the necessary training with the Spiritualist National Union. I'm currently doing a teaching course with the SNU at the Barbanell Centre, and I've also completed a mentoring course with the English medium Chris Drew, which enabled me to pass my Certificate of Spiritualist National Union in Speaking and Demonstrating.

I've been extremely lucky with the generous support I have been shown along my mediumship development journey, and all my family and friends have been extremely accepting and supportive of what I do as a working medium and healer. In March 2020, my youngest daughter, Rebekah, and I set out on a dream holiday to Florida in the United States. Unfortunately, because of the Covid-19 pandemic that had gripped the world the unimaginable happened and while Rebekah and I were mid-air the United States closed its borders to all United Kingdom travellers. Thankfully, because of these unique circumstances we were allowed entry, but we had our eight-day trip cut short to only four days while return flights were sought and found by our travel agent. I was, however, able to live out my dream and I performed a mediumship demonstration at the Cassadaga Spiritualist Camp in Florida.

I had previously met an American student at one of my many weeks at Arthur Findlay. This fellow student was from Florida, and they invited me to do a platform demonstration with them. I had read about this incredible-sounding place, and it was such a wonderful opportunity to demonstrate there as a medium, especially given I had only been developing my abilities since 2012. My demonstration was the day before we returned home to the United Kingdom, and I plan to return to the States to teach at Camp Cassadaga, as I've been invited to come back to do so.

After losing Charlene my mediumship has given me so much hope and the firm and unwavering belief in the continuation of 'life after life'; there is no such thing as death. I have been very fortunate as I haven't faced any difficulties with my mediumship; it just presented itself when I really needed it. Knowing I have been able to assist many other grieving people, just as I was helped in 2012 by the visiting medium, means the world to me.

My own death doesn't frighten me at all. I know I will be reunited with Charlene. Though having said this, I still want to live a long, full and happy life here with my family, and I know that in the interim Charlene is still with us all and will be there for me when my own mortal life ends and my next one in spirit begins.

I've had numerous challenges and much sadness in my lifetime, but I've also experienced many happy and amazing opportunities along the way, and I feel in many ways I'm just getting started. I regard myself as a very normal person who has been lucky enough to discover some wonderful and special abilities within myself that were always there.

Life is very busy. I work with Guy at our family-owned newsagency in Walton-on-Thames. I run two weekly mediumship teaching circles, and I do one-on-one readings from home in person and via Skype. I continue to give mediumship platform readings at the Hampton Hill Spiritual Church, where I am now the vice-president, and my mediumship studies continue. Life is good.

Newsagent and medium
Age, 53
Walton-on-Thames, United Kingdom

www.pamelapollington.co.uk
pam_pollington@msn.com

Chapter six

CHRISTEL ROSENKILDE CHRISTENSEN

Christel was first introduced to me by my friend, Toni Reilly, when she was visiting Australia from her native Denmark. Christel works independently with international corporations, companies and high-profile families as a facilitator, where she teaches those in senior positions and upper management how to work successfully with energy. Christel's aim is to achieve optimum results in the business and private lives of her many clients. I wanted to include Christel's amazing narrative because though she is a medium, she chooses to expand beyond those abilities further in her work and does so in a way that is both remarkable and unique. Christel is currently based in Denmark and has worked and lived internationally in many countries. She is also the author of *The Treasure: how to change the world.*

As a child I remember seeing and sensing energy around me, and my connection to this energy was as strong as seeing colour and physical things in the world. To me it has never felt spooky or different, just the most beautiful and expansive guiding light. I already had a knowing about the possibility of changing the energy of my own physical environment, and I understood the potential of communicating with the non-physical realm.

I was born and raised in the western part of Denmark, and since finishing my studies and leaving home I have lived and worked in three different continents and six different countries, being England, Belgium, France, the United States, China and Scotland. I am a very keen traveller and explorer of life.

I was raised in a family that upheld very strong values, morals and the importance of reliability and trust. My paternal grandparents were highly involved in the Lutheran Church. I happily attended all types of Christian holiday camps that were arranged by them, and I really enjoyed going. When I was around my grandparents I loved listening to the stories about Jesus and his healing capacity and ability to create miracles. I understood and believed in the principles and values that were shared in the children's version of the Bible; hence the stories of a man who inspired a new world seemed to resonate with me, and the religious dogma escaped my attention.

At home we didn't practise religion as a part of life; however, we were made very aware of the suffering of others less fortunate in the world and how much of this hardship was unnecessary. My mother came from a family where love and family was the main priority. Her family were atheists, and yet again the focus was to care for others as the most important deed anyone could do in life. My mother's side of the family were typical working-class people; her father was a self-employed hairdresser and a talented musician who played the violin and trumpet, and he inspired me to learn several different instruments and to sing. I always felt fully supported, and my grandparents' unconditional love for me was very evident. I was praised for being different in my thinking, which made me never question myself and the unique way I walked in life.

My parents built a very stable life for our family. My father was the managing director of a toy company, and my mother worked with him part-time, so she could be with us children after school. At dinnertime, me and my two younger brothers would listen to our parents talking about the management of the company, workplace issues and reassessing what happened that day in the family business. My parents were always talking from a place where I could gain an early insight into corporate and leadership challenges and solutions.

My father was adamant that we spent time in nature, and our weekly family walks in the forest became like a form of healing for me. The forest and garden created a sense of peace; I saw energies around the trees, and I felt the unseen spirits that were around me in nature. It was always apparent to me that most people didn't 'see' things as I did. The sereneness that many find in nature wasn't always the case for me, and as a child the forest was a scary place to be alone in. What wasn't seen with my physical eyes was very much felt in every cell inside my body, and now science has proven that trees communicate and they have their own energy and a heartbeat, it's slow, but it's there; and I felt it.

As a teenager I was highly determined to train hard and do well in my chosen sports, firstly competitive swimming and later karate, in which I competed at national and international levels. I was fascinated by the physical and mindful potential of both sporting pursuits, and I learnt to appreciate the combination of meditation, the focus of the mind and the physical application of a visualised practice. I also learnt how to use my intuitive gift to detect when danger was coming from behind in a karate match and how to 'know' a competitor's next move.

For me dreams have always been like a portal to the universe and always very significant; they have often warned me when something dire was about to happen. When I was eleven years old I dreamt that my grandfather died. It was all so clear to me, and I woke up very upset by what I had experienced. I went into my parents' bedroom to tell them what had happened, and they told me to go back to bed and forget about my dream. The next morning the phone rang, and my family received the terrible news that my grandfather had passed during the night, just as I had 'seen'. I have always cherished the 'knowing' that he told me he was dying, and I feel that he had come to say goodbye. My grandfather was a big part of my life as a child, and he still is today.

I started doing simple meditations at the age of ten, and these became more structured at around twelve. My grandmother had cancer at that time, and she was introduced to a self-healing class to complement her traditional cancer treatment. This new type of therapy involved meditation, and her teacher had also recorded a guided meditation tape specifically designed for children, which she gave to my grandmother. These guided meditations taught children how to believe in their own self-worth and to help strengthen their motivation and focus. I felt immediately at home listening to the tape for the very first time. It was also then that I began to be more aware of seeing, sensing, hearing, smelling and knowing about the changes in the energy around me, but on a much more conscious level.

As a teenager I used a ouija board with my friends. To us this was such an exciting thing to do. We would communicate with ghosts (as we called them) and write down the names of the spirit communicators that came through; then we would go to the local cemetery and verify their names and dates of death from the gravestones to see how accurate we were.

When I was twenty-three years old a friend told me about a weekend workshop that she thought would be perfect for me. This friend and I had studied international business studies together, and from the first day we met and started talking we realised we had both encountered different yet similar experiences relating to the spirit world. The weekend workshop she had suggested was called, 'Are you curious to see if you are clairvoyant?' All of the things listed on the pamphlet sounded very natural to me, and I felt a strong need to sign up and attend.

On the first day we did numerous exercises including energy awareness, psychic readings and psychometry. For me everything was easy, and I could do all the tasks successfully. This surprised my fellow students, my teacher and myself too. Being an academic, this puzzled me, yet everything was evidentially confirmed by the other participants who I was doing the readings for.

When we arrived on the second day the teacher was playing very dramatic music in the room. There were candles burning everywhere, and we were told we would be contacting and communicating with our deceased loved ones and studying mediumship. (To this day, I still don't agree with this type of dramatisation around mediumship; it's a natural process to be handled with love and respect, which I prefer to tap into undisturbed and without any theatrics.)

We were all asked to write the name of a loved one in spirit on a piece of paper, and these names were placed in a bowl. I was sceptical about what we were about to do, and I wasn't sure that I wanted to embark on this mediumship journey, as I didn't understand the purpose of this type of communication. I was scared to deliver a message to someone in the room from a deceased loved one, and I was mindful not to hurt anyone's feelings or to make someone feel uncomfortable. Little did I know at the time how healing a spirit communication could be.

I wasn't feeling comfortable at all, and I was ready to leave when the teacher asked me to at least try before abandoning my course. I agreed and picked a name from the bowl in the middle of the room. I tuned into the spirit world as instructed, and I instantly connected to a male spirit communicator. I could hear the age – twenty-seven years – and I knew he was the son of a participant in the room. I felt immediately shocked, and I broke down in tears. How could I continue and do this to his mother? I was imagining her sorrow. The teacher assured me that the mother had agreed to participate and maybe even wished for a communication with her son.

For teaching purposes we had all been instructed not to offer any information about our loved ones in spirit before the exercise began.

I tuned in again and set my own emotions on hold. The young man appeared again, and he was showing me that he had drowned under a huge wave and he kept showing me the brand of his T-shirt. I could see very clearly how he once looked in life, and I could describe his physical appearance, but I still didn't recognise the brand name on his T-shirt, so I described the imagery of it.

I conveyed a very personal memory he had shared with his mother and many other very clear pieces of information to show evidence of his survival into the spirit world. I was amazed when his mother confirmed all of the information I had given in the reading, and she then shared her story. Her son had tragically drowned during the shocking tsunami that hit Thailand in 2004. He had been travelling with his work, and the brand on his T-shirt was the logo of the company he worked for. His beautiful messages and the sharing of his love for his mother were so moving. It was so important for him to show that he was still around her and that he loved her greatly.

After the reading ended the mother said she felt healed and reassured – not to mention how the reading healed me too. The connection with this young man in spirit had instantly streamed through me with no effort on my part, and I knew then that I was a natural-born medium.

When one of my brothers was twenty-two years old, he almost died while he was on a climbing trek in Peru. No-one in my family had any knowledge of this, but I dreamt that he was in real danger, I just didn't know what from. Because my dream was so real to me, when I woke I emailed my mother to ask if everything was all right and if she had heard anything from him. Weeks later we were told by my brother that he had a terrible case of altitude sickness, and it had been life threatening for him. I knew from my dream that my concern about him was very real, and it made me instinctively send healing energies to him, allowing me to assist him energetically right when he needed someone or something extra to survive his ordeal.

As a student I didn't know my future path, but I was attracted to certain topics at school, and I feel I had been divinely guided to select the subjects I did. I didn't know it then, but now I see the reason for my choices. I studied double degrees in both international negotiation and international management and ethics and sustainability and global entrepreneurship at various universities and business schools around the world, and later I did some self-studies into learning about and understanding quantum physics.

At a very young age I was privileged to work in an international management position for a large corporation based in Shanghai, China. The company had clients in forty-five countries, and a part of my role was to travel the world to gain experience and knowledge about international business. My life living in Shanghai was very much a life of luxury, with the whole jet-setting expatriate lifestyle; I honestly thought I loved it.

My mother rang me unexpectedly from Denmark to say that my younger brother had been detected with heart failure (he is thankfully fine today), and all I wanted to do was to go home to be with my family. The same week I heard my brother's worrying news, all of us expatriates working for the company were to be assessed by an external expatriate coach. It was a global requirement of the company to have these assessments done to ensure that all the team were in the best physical and mental condition possible, in order to be at their best in the workplace. We had to answer a whole series of verbal questions, and when I was asked if I was happy in my role, I immediately answered yes.

Initially I felt that this was all a waste of time, but later on in the session the coach asked me what was important to me. My answers were family, friends, nature, time to live and see people, time for myself, doing good in the world … these are the things that are essential for me to have in order to live a happy and fulfilling life. It was as if something exploded within me, and I realised that my answer to the first question was wrong. I loved the experiences I was having and the freedom my position gave me to travel and have financial stability, but I realised that the most essential things were missing in my world. I knew I had to take control and make some very significant changes in my life, so I phoned my mother and said I was coming home. The following week I resigned from my dream job and I moved back to Denmark.

Each day after returning home to my family I would set my intention to receive clarity about certain issues that concerned me, and I would meditate. I wanted to know why I had the academic background and the work experience that I had. I was questioning the value of any of it and why had it had taken me so far from everything that was so important to me. Then slowly I began to see the 'gift' in all of the experiences I had been a part of during my time working in China; I heard the words, 'Apply it to make the world a better place.'

As a direct result of my meditation, I developed the concept of Energistic Leadership (I own the patent for this brand name, hence the unusual spelling), a unique program that allowed me to communicate and teach executive groups in the business sector. I share with them the power of thought, choices and actions, the ripple effect of energy, and demonstrate the responsibility and capacity we all have within us to change things on a global level with our own energy.

My primary focus was to make people conscious of how we, as individuals, have more power within us to change things for the better than we realise. If our energies, our thoughts, our choices and actions are aligned and we become aware of what is preventing us from reaching our highest and most impactful potential, then we all have the capacity to perform small and big miracles every single day. It is my work and my passion to make this happen for others.

I followed my own guidance in building my new business concept, and I started my company in 2007. At the time of launching my new venture the global financial crisis was looming and it hit the following year, making it a very challenging time for myself and everyone globally in business. During my meditations I was told not to promote myself far and wide but only to a select few specific networks of business executives. I was guided to use my own energy to organically 'attract' the clients and business I needed and nothing more. Shortly afterwards a business leader called me from Switzerland wanting to engage my services and, not long after, other executives who had heard me speak at business events began calling me as well. It was a slow build, and quite magically my company survived the financial crisis and came out stronger than I could have ever imagined.

In my everyday work I assist chief executive officers, business owners, athletes, spiritual advisers and many other different kinds of clients in reaching their highest potential in their businesses. My role will often require assessments of executive teams, strategies and optimisation of day-to-day practices. My work also involves firefighting and troubleshooting different aspects of the business and working with those in senior management, who are responsible for the departments in question.

My personal insights into the corporate world at such a high level have given me the much-needed wisdom for the work that I do now in my business, and I have a real understanding of the challenges and daily tasks that my corporate executive clients deal with. I use this know-how to support them in the best possible manner. At other times I guide my clients in clarifying and understanding the needs of their children, to optimise their personal relationships and to help improve their family life as a result. I determine what is holding them back from living their greatest lives and achieving their highest potential in their private life and in their work performance.

I assist my professional athlete clients to find their deeper sense of purpose, using their fame and success to ripple and communicate a deeper message to their following. I see their potential and blockages, both physically and mentally, and I ease their stress and help them to heal from injuries, so they can once again excel in their chosen sports. I teach my clients in workshop situations to reach a greater personal level of power so they can influence, improve and create better personal results and in doing so change the world and their work environment for the better.

To give an example of how my business works, about six years ago I received a totally unexpected phone call from the CEO of a global corporation in the United States. This executive had just attended a charity dinner in Chicago, and he had sat next to an extremely influential government adviser who was involved in finance for the United States. This adviser had spoken to a previous client of mine in Australia, who explained how I had worked with him on his personal leadership and how I also helped his team in some important decision-making processes and strategies. These findings were implemented to advance their company in a very positive way. My caller was fascinated by this story, and he felt that it was extraordinary that high-level companies used an intuitive adviser to make transformations for their company.

During our phone call the CEO said that no matter the cost I was needed in the United States to speak at the company's leadership workshop, which was scheduled in three weeks time. Prior to being flown over in first class I was sent a special security clearance letter to present at customs on arrival. When I landed the customs officers were asking me, 'Who are you?' because of the importance of the security letter and who it was signed by.

At my workshops I always work intuitively by psychically tuning in on the companies' strategies and challenges and their obvious advantages as well, which could advance the company. I also use my own academic and global working experiences, together with my intuitive information, to formulate a workshop that is totally unique to each client; none are ever the same. As a part of my strategy, I show them how as individuals they can influence the energies of others, and in doing so they can change their own perspectives from being fearful and results-focused to being more uplifting, thereby creating a shared purpose for themselves and for their clients, essentially optimising their entire stakeholder chain.

At this leadership workshop all of the team leaders were highly religious, and they were observing me very closely. Part of my work is always a combination of group work and one-on-one consultations with the company executives. In the one-on-one sessions, the first man arrived to meet me and we had a wonderful discussion about his strengths and weakness, and I determined where I could help him with his individual challenges and how to enhance his leadership skills, at both work and in his private life. We also spent quite some time talking about his religious faith and how this could be applied and funnelled into his work. When he left he said, 'You know why I was the first person here? Because they all trusted me to find out if you are the devil-messenger or if you truly came here with God.'

If that man had said no to his colleagues, then none of them would have come to have their one-on-one interviews with me, but thankfully they all did. So strong were their religious beliefs that all of the executives were concerned that I was going to 'put the devil on their shoulder' if I wasn't legitimate. This experience allowed me to understand that in business, every company with a very strong religious background would be heavily scrutinising me to see that I wasn't sent by the devil! After the initial workshop I started working with this company for years, and I even created a special guided meditation for the executives. The company arranged for the meditation to be recorded properly in a recording studio, and they sent my meditation out to all of their executive staff around the world.

I was once flown to China by this same client for an extremely important negotiation relating to a billion-dollar merger between two large companies, one being Chinese and the other American. I was introduced by my client as their 'spiritual adviser and mystic', who would be having the final decision-making power about whether the merger would take place or not. I was to use my abilities in the capacity of 'the Illuminator' and to rate the potential for success in each party. Of course, everyone present feared or hoped I would speak for their respective case in my conclusion.

I have also worked with Emirate Royals, guiding them to transform their roles into being more positive and assisting them with everything from personal and business coaching, enhancing their faith and commitment to a better spiritual understanding and connection, and thereby allowing them to change things for the better in their everyday challenges and work.

When working with teams I often experience resistance to the way that I work when I'm first introduced by the CEO or leader of the team. Most of my clients tend to be men, and I believe that the initial contention exists because I come from a perspective that most have never considered before, and all are afraid to have their inner life and insecurities revealed. There are always disbelievers present in every instance, and some even question if the CEO has actually lost his mind. I've had situations where some executives absolutely resent the approach I have and they are intent on initially destroying the workshop, but they always stay for the whole two days once we start work.

When working with a group I make sure to only intuit and communicate what enhances the individual, and I never reveal negatives or put people down in front of a group. My goal is always to build and empower the team and its members. Of course, in the one-on-one meetings, I confront the needed challenges, and if damaging for the company, I of course need to make the leader aware so they can take the necessary actions in maintaining the best team possible. I also assist in hiring key players for important roles or projects.

In my consulting work I use mediumship on a very discretionary level and only if spirit communication is needed to assist my client to release and heal something within. If I 'know' they need to receive a specific message from a loved one in spirit, then I will share that. For me mediumship is just one part of my multifaceted spiritual gifts that I use to assist my clients.

About ten years ago, I decided to attend a course for the first time at the Arthur Findlay College in the United Kingdom. I have since returned many times to the college to attune my mediumship abilities and to be around people with similar capabilities and gifts to myself. It was here I started to learn more about the importance of working with evidence of survival into the spirit world, when I was working with a spirit communicator. Seeing and understanding the importance of giving evidence when communicating made me also see the relevance of delivering specific information to my clients when illuminating their challenges and opportunities in their businesses.

As a medium, maintaining old friendships can sometimes be difficult. I still have friends who date back to my childhood and early twenties, yet I have also said goodbye to best friends and people I thought I would never to let go of. As intuitive people we always sense dishonesty or when things are simply not right. Maybe we don't always know exactly what it is, but we do have a very real knowing that something is not right in a relationship and therefore it can't continue.

Because I am very aware of reading the energy of people, romantic relationships can sometimes be very difficult. Years ago I had started dating a man, and one afternoon out of nowhere, I had a flash of information and I could see him talking on the phone with his wife. When speaking with him later I confronted him about this, and he told me that he had never divorced his wife and they were still married. Of course, that relationship ended immediately, and I give thanks to my strong intuition for alerting me.

In 2017 I took maternity leave to give birth to my daughter, Chloe, who is a true blessing to me. My daughter's father and I have been separated for some time now, and he recently asked me to consider reuniting. We are very different as people, but for my daughter's sake I promised to reconsider getting back together with him, as a family. I didn't take his offer lightly and, despite the daily messages from him proclaiming his love for me, I dreamt that he was seeing someone else. After I woke up I messaged him, only to have him confirm what I already knew. He is very aware of my abilities, and he knew not to try and keep up his lie.

My dream allowed me to finally let go of any doubts I had for our daughter's future, and I felt no guilt in knowing that we are never going to be together and we could now both move forward separately with our lives. Again the insight was a gift, reassuring me that moving forward separately was the right thing for all parties.

I know that many men also do mediumship, but the general misconception is that only women are mediums. As in all vocations, there are experienced and well-trained mediums who are continually working on their self-development and self-awareness. These people are ethical and true to the needs of their clients and not a servant to their own ego. Sadly, there are also many outright frauds when it comes to mediumship, including some innocent people who desire and believe themselves to have the ability of mediumship but don't.

The work we do as mediums matters more than we may know, and to me our mediumistic abilities are all about healing and empowering people to be aware that they matter and to know there is always a way forward that gives them hope. We tap into to the immense energies that are so much greater than ourselves, and once we do this we can shine our light and make a difference in helping those who grieve. I accept the lack of understanding that exists universally about mediumship. I usually say I work in the gap between what meets the eye, science, the tangible world and faith … in between, there is a gap, and this is where all the magic lives and where miracles are created.

I don't practise a specific religion myself, but I do feel the presence of a divine Source. I was baptised and confirmed as a Christian Protestant, yet wherever I am in the world I can enter a religious church or temple and connect to Source, to God, and I have the deepest respect for all religions. As a part of my work, I assist people from all walks of life to connect and strengthen their communication to their own interpretation of God, and I now have a list of clients from twenty-eight countries around the world, so their religious and spiritual beliefs are very mixed and varied.

On 1 October 2019 in a recording for my *Treasure Visionary Guidance* website and later shared on YouTube, I talked about a specific date that I was 'given', and I shared this in the recording. I had foreseen that around 20 March in 2020, we would experience a significant happening that would change our world. It would be the start of a conscious revolution that would change our lives beyond our understanding, and each one of us had to be prepared somehow. Little did I know that this warning was the exact date when many countries began a complete lockdown due to Covid-19. A virus that has changed the way we live and a lockdown that shows us how nature thrives when we are polluting less, travelling less and disturbing the natural world less. A virus that makes us all navigate the world differently and will not leave us, or the world looking in the same way. We are forever changed, and we will see a new world transpire, not only due to Covid-19, but certainly triggered by it. We will look back in ten years from now to see what significant changes have happened.

Medium, world leader adviser, spiritual teacher, energy expert
Age, 42
Denmark

crc@treasureworldleaders.com
www.christelrosenkildechristensen.com

Chapter seven

Toni Reilly

Toni has played a huge role in my psychic and mediumship development, and she ran the first spiritual development circle I joined, in early 2014. Toni is curious by nature, and she embraces every opportunity to learn more about what interests her. She is courageous, as you will learn from her story, and Toni is intent on helping people understand their life's true purpose. Though adept in many modalities of the psychic sciences, Toni's obvious passion is in her past-life regression work. Toni is Australian, and she is currently living in Queensland. Toni's work takes her Australia-wide and internationally. Her memoir, *Awake: The Purpose of Life and Why You Are Here*, is a number one bestseller on Amazon.

My beginnings are a stark contrast to the life that I have experienced since. I was born in Cowra in New South Wales, a small town 300 kilometres west of Sydney in Australia. My father, Bruce, was a truck driver, and my mother, Wendy, was a stay-at-home mum, taking care of my older sister, Linda, and my younger brother, Bruce. I started primary school in Cowra, and I absolutely hated it. I had no friends; I didn't seem to fit in, and I feel that my lifelong sense of insecurity developed at this very early stage of my life. I was totally relieved and excited when my parents said we were leaving the area to live at a mining construction site in the state of Queensland, where Dad had a new job.

Like all mining towns, the school and other amenities are built literally in the middle of nowhere, and all of the workers' children are schooled in these new makeshift buildings. Life in the mining towns was extremely remote. The surroundings were desolate, and it always seemed to be so hot and dusty. Dad was working on road construction gangs who were tasked with creating the new road system in desolate places in northern Queensland, and the work was physically tough.

As a child it was initially exciting to start living somewhere new and to move around from mining town to mining town, but sometimes it was difficult because as soon as I might manage to make a new friend, it was time to move on again to another construction site and another school. My schooling could only be described as spasmodic; I attended nine different schools in total, and when I turned fourteen I couldn't wait to leave. In my first year of high school, I was taught by mail correspondence, so I had no face-to-face interaction with any of my teachers or with any of my co-students, and I loved it!

My education was also hampered by the different school systems and age criteria that existed between the states of New South Wales and Queensland. Once we left Cowra, I was automatically put up a year, making me always the youngest student in the grade, but I felt smart being in with the older kids. By law I could leave school at year ten level; I was fourteen at that stage, and this was fine by my parents, but only if I was able find work and be financially independent. My first job was selling bread and cakes at the local bakery in Glenden, and then I started working at the town's only supermarket. I wanted to broaden my opportunities in life, so I left Glenden and moved to Mackay in northern Queensland where I did administrative work at the local newspaper, *The Daily Mercury*.

At twenty, I had met my future husband, and we married when I was twenty-four, and we had three fantastic children in quick succession: our daughter, Bebe; son, Reo; and another daughter, Coco. By this stage, my husband and I were now living in Brisbane, and it was during this time that I found I was very drawn to all things of a spiritual nature. I didn't do anything about my new-found interest, because my husband made me feel foolish if I talked about it in any way. I intuitively believed in unseen phenomena, even though I had no understanding of how psychic things worked. That I may possess psychic abilities of my own didn't really occur to me, as I was so busy with my everyday life, working part-time and looking after our three small children.

My husband and I were very different as people, which can often work to your advantage, but this wasn't the case for us, and although we were together for sixteen years, our marriage didn't survive. I was in my mid-thirties when we separated, and for the first time I finally felt free to do something about learning about my own intuitive strengths. I feel that my psychic abilities really presented themselves and boomed after leaving my husband, and at last I was able to pursue my own interests.

Not long afterwards my life became very busy and also quite complex; I met a new partner, who lived and worked in Melbourne. Thankfully, my now ex-husband and I could agree to share co-parenting of the children on alternative weeks, and for the next eight years I commuted by plane the 1,775 kilometres between Brisbane and Melbourne. When I was back in Brisbane I worked part-time at an Aboriginal art gallery that was owned by my sister-in-law (my ex-husband's sister) and her husband. We had always gotten along well, and thankfully this never changed, even after our divorce.

During my alternate weeks in Melbourne I had plenty of spare time for myself, as my partner was working full-time, so I made it my mission to join a spiritual development circle, which I found quite randomly on the internet. My teacher was extremely helpful, and through her I began to meditate, which led me to discover many very personal aspects about myself that I previously wasn't aware of. These insights allowed me to fully examine who I was as a person, and they gave me much-needed clarity in where my future life would take me.

I loved my weekly development sessions, and I became addicted to my circle group. Meditating came very easily to me, as did reading Tarot cards. I knew I had discovered a whole new way to move forward with my life. I became very competent with reading Tarot cards, and on the alternate weeks when I was back home looking after my three children, I began working regularly as a Tarot card reader in a shop in Brisbane, and I gave up my job at the art gallery.

The spiritual teacher at my Melbourne circle had told me about a book called *Many Lives, Many Masters* by Dr Brian Weiss, an American psychiatrist. She suggested I read it, as she felt that many of my own issues stemmed from previous encounters in my past lives. I was fascinated by this possibility, and after finally locating a copy of the book I learnt that Dr Weiss had inadvertently discovered that past lives could be accessed through hypnosis, and these previous lifetimes held extraordinary healing powers for the patient once they were reawakened and examined.

After reading the book, I decided to have my own past-life regression session with a practitioner who was referred to me by my teacher, and it was life changing for me. Soon after I began training in past-life regression therapy in Melbourne, I completed my studies and began working with my own clients in this rather unusual but fascinating field. My spiritual development study became my work focus, and I made the decision to dedicate myself to become self-employed with my intuitive Tarot readings and past-life regression therapy.

After running my business for over a year I wanted to learn more, so I flew to the United States to do a training course about past-life regression at the Omega Centre in New York with Dr Brian Weiss. During the course I observed that Dr Weiss had a very clinical way of training us, but I also understood that this stemmed from his own very science-based training as a practising psychiatrist. I regard Dr Weiss as my mentor, and I was privileged to go on television with him when I was in in the States. I was invited to be a guest on his Australian tour soon afterwards.

When I was in Melbourne for my alternate week, I worked very much on building a business profile for myself, and this became a real focus for me. In 2008 I created a training program of my own, which was designed to train students about past-life regression, how it worked and the benefits of using it. To do this I started to work with groups and run workshops all over Australia and internationally to share my knowledge. I wanted to make past-life regression more mainstream, so that people could utilise it to help them deal with emotional, physical and mental symptoms. Even to me, it sounded like a weird thing to be training people in, but I saw the healing potential, which borders on miraculous.

I founded the Toni Reilly Institute as a recognised teaching facility for past-life regression therapy in 2009. It was important for me to offer students the opportunity to access the benefits of experiencing past-life regression therapy, as I knew it worked so well with my own clients. The people who came to me for past-life regression would be there for many reasons, including anxiety, grief, heartbreak, recurring relationship issues, fear of flying, fear of lifts, fear of public speaking and many others. I used to call it the psychology of the future, but now I call it the psychology of NOW, because of how consistently it clears issues.

My SoulLife Coaching certification is a system for personal development. There are various components to my recall regression course, and it includes intuitive counselling (written by Pamela Ray), intuition development and a simplified personality and life outline map system, which I call 'SoulLife Map – Your Life Mission Master Plan'. I believe the most important aspect of anyone working with others is understanding self-awareness. We all have 'stuff', and knowing what it is stops us from placing it on others. Therefore, my programs and training are all experiential, so that in the process of learning to work with others, you also work on yourself.

On my weeks back in Brisbane, I attended another development circle run by a wonderful woman called Pamela Ray, who was not only a very gifted teacher but also a qualified psychotherapist, counsellor and medium, which I found to be an interesting combination. We became close. Pamela was twenty years older than me; we met when she was sixty and I was forty. I soon discovered that Pamela had been in a similar situation to me twenty years previously: her own messy marriage had broken up, and she was on her own search spiritually. When I joined Pamela's circle, I was completely unaware of my own mediumship abilities, as I had been focusing solely on psychic development in my Melbourne classes, and we had not done anything at all to do with mediumship. I absolutely believed in the existence of the spirit world. I wanted to know more about mediumship, and I knew that Pamela was the right person to help me.

I feel blessed to have met Pamela, and she was integral in the many changes that my life was about to take. At Pamela's development circle, she talked about how she and her second husband had lived in London in the late eighties and early nineties, and during that time they had both attended classes at a place called Arthur Findlay College. I had never heard of it, but I knew I had to go there. Pamela and her husband had both been fortunate enough to train at the college with the renowned Gordon Higginson, who I also knew nothing about. Pamela was lucky enough to also work with other English mediums, Mavis Pitilla and Paul Jacobs, and both had a profound and positive effect on her development as a medium.

Pamela always talked about the importance of training properly at the very beginning of developing your mediumship abilities, so in 2009 I flew to the United Kingdom and had a phenomenal week studying mediumship for the very first time. Thanks to the wonderful tutors who taught me on that week, I managed to make my first connection with spirit, and I could communicate with the loved ones of the other students in my class.

Following my first experience studying at Arthur Findlay College, I knew without a doubt that mediumship was indeed very real, and after being put to the test many times, I realised also that I was a medium. Since that first amazing trip, I have returned for further weekly study on another three separate occasions.

In my work I love being the facilitator who teaches others to work in past-life regression therapy or to help students to develop any mediumship and psychic abilities they may have. I love sharing my knowledge with others and seeing my students discover and utilise their own untapped skills. The work that I do is all energy based, and my aim is to empower both students and clients, so I can bring clarity and calmness to people's lives. One key focus of my work is spruiking the benefits of mediumship as a means of helping people deal with their own grief. The healing powers of being able to reconnect them with a loved one in spirit are immeasurable.

When I was thirty-eight, I started writing my own life story, and I called it *Awake: The Purpose of Life and Why You Are Here.* It took me eight years to complete the manuscript and to get it published. I know it was meant to take that long, as so many changes were happening along the way in my own life, and these needed to be reflected in the actual book. The greatest personal gift of all my meditating and development work is my self-awareness, which I truly believe is the key to living a contented life.

After working with thousands of clients and students, I observed and started to understand that our lives are pre-set and outlined already, so I wrote Awake to showcase what I perceived about my own life and what I had experienced so far in my journey. It allowed me to see why I was born into the family that I was, and it gave me clarity about the people who were in my life and why they appeared when they did. I believe everything in life is predestined and pre-mapped, and these things are what our life's purpose is.

All of my children are very supportive of what I do. My work is very normal for them, and each one has enormous potential to develop as mediums in the future, if that is their wish. My mother has always been very psychic, and I was aware of this as I was growing up. She would just know things intuitively, and though Mum doesn't practise anything herself, she is open to the reality of both psychic and mediumship communications. Dad is also very intuitive, but he's not really into the subject of psychic phenomena, though he's fine with others being interested.

I always find it interesting why people initially contact mediums and psychics for a reading. Many people don't think too deeply about life until something horrible happens to them, such as the passing of a loved one or heartbreak from a broken relationship. Only then, through trauma, do they start to look for the deeper meaning of life and seek out mediums, psychics and healers to provide answers and a way to cope.

Certainly not everyone seeks solace via mediums, and I know that mediumship is considered taboo for many people. I feel this has a lot to do with the way it's portrayed in the Hollywood movies. All too often, movies and TV shows create a lot of ridiculous hype and imaginary scenarios that make everything related to mediumship appear silly. I'm not a fan of the fluffy, witchy-woo aspect to how people wrongly perceive and interpret what mediums and psychics do.

Through the natural evolution of humanity the energy of the world has changed and, extraordinarily, through my years of work I see that people are naturally more in tune to energy and curious about intuition. I feel that our young people are born more sensitive, and this is a beautiful thing.

Society, cultural beliefs and religion all have a lot to do with shaping people's beliefs and misunderstandings about what's considered acceptable and mainstream. It's also often the case that people are parroting what their own parents have taught them, and they have been conditioned to fear and be suspicious of anything that is remotely spiritual. It's only the people who have had a positive experience with a medium who understand the wonderful healing that follows a successful mediumship reading or recall regression session. My mission has always been to make mediumship and all forms of energy work more mainstream and acceptable. I want the general population to understand how beneficial these types of sessions are and how they can help people in ways that traditional therapies and medicine can't.

I find it interesting that there are often differing beliefs among mediums about certain practices, and I think it's important to raise them here. Without a shred of doubt, I believe that the spirit world is pure, safe and non-threatening in any way. Simply put, it is not scary. Yet when I first started studying mediumship, I was alarmed by mediums who kept talking about protecting themselves from the spirit world. No protection is needed, nothing can or will harm you; it's just dangerous and careless misinformation. The fearmongering continues with talk about people having 'attachments' connected to them, and I want people to understand that nothing can attach itself to you. Energy is universal, a collective that we are all part of. Understanding how it works and how attuned we are is the best way to reduce unwarranted fear.

With the work that I primarily do, I'm essentially working with 'death', as my role is to regress my clients and students to allow them to experience their own past lives and subsequent passing in that life. I have been regressed many times myself, and I know firsthand the wonders of seeing where and how I lived at another time, in another place. Because of my work I'm not scared to die when my time comes, as I already know what it's like to take that last breath, and I can tell you there is very little separation between this life and the afterlife.

I also believe that in life we have an 'in date' and an 'out date'; they are all pre-set. Your date of birth, your day of entry into your new life is set, and you are to be born on that predetermined date, regardless of whether you are premature or overdue; you always arrive when you were meant to. Likewise, you cannot leave your life before your time, even in the event of suicide. It was always going to be the date that you were to die, or as I like to call it, transition home. I see death as the spirit transitioning from the physical body back to pure energy.

So far in my own life I have not lost many loved ones, with the exception of my grandparents and my dear friend Pamela Ray, who passed in 2018. During my numerous weeks at Arthur Findlay College, each of my grandparents have come through in one-on-one readings with fellow students, and I love having a complete stranger make these beautiful communications for me. When we lose loved ones, I believe it's those left behind who suffer most, because of our immense love for that person. It's certainly not the person in spirit, as they have a wonderful experience ahead of them. For Pamela, her death was very sudden: she had experienced some lower back pain, so she went to see her doctor, who immediately did some tests. She died just eleven days later from cancer; it was all through her body. Pamela and I spent a lot of time talking after her prognosis was given, and we were very open in our discussions.

I know and understand a lot about death, but I was sad, and my normal human emotions said that it was unfair. Pamela was initially scared to die; it was the reality of leaving her loved ones behind. After all of Pamela's work as a medium during her lifetime and the number of spirit communications she had made for others, she was still curious and slightly nervous about going to the afterlife.

Pamela's husband had passed away just eight months beforehand, and he initially had been really scared about dying, even though he was also a medium. Just prior to their respective deaths, both came to terms and found peace in the knowledge and understanding of the continuation of life after a physical death, but they both independently felt it was unfair to die before they had lived to a very old age. This showed me that regardless of all our knowledge and beliefs, we are all just normal people with normal fears about the final unknown.

Being a medium and working in a field that is not widely understood makes me mindful of telling strangers what I do, and I always use my intuition before telling new people how I make a living. I'm a sensitive person; I value my work, and I never treat it like a sideshow or as entertainment. If I feel that the new person won't understand what I do regarding my work, I say that I am a counsellor and I don't mention mediumship or past lives.

I didn't receive negative comments from any of my friends regarding what I do with my work when I first started posting things online. Because my interest in mediumship came to me later in life, I was mindful what my old friends may think of my new turn in life, but many of them were very interested in mediumship themselves, which I took as a magical synchronicity. I'm not interested in converting anyone; I share the information, my philosophies and case studies, so people can take it or leave it.

Religion was not a big part of my upbringing, so I don't regard myself as a religious person. My mother is not at all religious, whereas my father was raised Catholic and he wanted all of us children to be christened in the Catholic Church, though that was the full extent of our religious education. In Dad's extended family there are Catholic priests, but other members of his family don't practise religion at all. My father had a tragic childhood: his mother was killed in a car accident when he was just one year old, and he was sitting on her lap when she died. Dad was raised by his older brothers and father, and when he was a baby, his brothers hid him in a cupboard when the priest came to the door, as they knew he wanted to place Dad into an orphanage. Dad was sent to a Catholic school, where he and his friends were constantly and brutally caned by the nuns.

I feel that something untoward happened to my maternal grandfather, concerning the priests, during his own childhood. I say this because he would always warn my mother when she was going to school to not go near the priests. In my late grandfather's eyes, there was a dislike of the Church and those who represented it, and these negative feelings remain deeply ingrained with my mother.

One of the schools I attended was a Catholic primary school. There was a very cruel female teacher who wasn't a nun, but she was downright nasty and violent. I could never understand this, for religion is supposed to be caring and kind, but that wasn't my experience at all. At another school, when I was eleven years old, a priest visited and asked all of us children if our parents were christened or not. I said that my mother wasn't christened, and he told me that I must go home and tell my mother to get christened or she would go to hell! This played on my mind for years and really worried me, and even though I was young, I reflected on how wrong it was to put such fears into the minds of innocent children. It made me question the validity of organised religion. My own belief is that God is the culmination of all our combined energies. It's not one energy that's above us; we are a part of the same collective energy that we call 'God' or 'the universe' or 'soul energy'.

Being self-employed and working in an area that is not exactly mainstream has been financially difficult to do by myself. After my husband and I divorced, I received an almost unencumbered house in the property settlement, and I always managed to make enough money to build my business, pay for my mediumship studies overseas and provide for my children. After my second relationship ended, I decided to sell my Brisbane house and use the proceeds to help build and promote my business. In the end, I invested every dollar from the property sale into creating content and programs to teach people.

I trust my vision, and I continually work towards the tipping point when the whole thing impacts people globally. Through the Toni Reilly Institute and SoulLife Map, I know I have discovered a way to teach people of any age about their true value and to help them overcome insecurities and raise their self-worth, so they do not feel like victims of life and instead embrace their purpose in every experience.

I feel grateful for the magical and unbelievable experiences that I have had so far. My work has taken me to many places around the world, including Denmark, Scotland, the United Kingdom,

India, New Zealand and the United States, and many of these places I've visited on numerous occasions. However, I don't do much mediumship work now, because I love to facilitate clients to connect with their loved one themselves. A few years ago, I was part of a mediumship demonstration tour with two mediums I had met at Arthur Findlay. One of the mediums was an American, the other was English, and we did mediumship platform demonstrations in Chicago and Atlanta. I love the power you feel in platform demonstrations, but it takes a lot of courage to get up and do it.

The focus of my work these days is writing the content for my LifeMap system and book. I also have a podcast called *Life Map*. Prior to Covid-19, I was in New York, Aspen and Los Angeles performing regression therapy for clients and also in Denmark researching and verifying my past-life recollections there; this is part of a series of documented past-life cases that will feature as a documentary series.

Life is grand. I feel like we are here on Earth to enjoy this wonderful thing called life, and I am having fun and making the most of it, and I wish that for you too.

Self-awareness is the ultimate activism.

Past-life regression counsellor and medium
Age, 50
Queensland, Australia

www.tonireillyinstitute.com
toni@tonireillyinstitute.com

Chapter eight

LORRAINE CULROSS

Lorraine was the first medium who Sergio and I visited, a mere six weeks after Sam's accident in 2012. Lorraine first introduced me to the wonders of mediumship, something I had no knowledge of at the time. I believed in life after death – the continuation of life in spirit form – but that was all I knew. Lorraine's reading was a powerful and healing experience that altered many aspects of my own life and, in many ways, me. It seems only fitting that Lorraine share her own pathway to mediumship in these pages, and I'm so glad we met and have become good friends. Lorraine is Australian and lives in regional Victoria, in the old gold mining town of Ballarat.

I was born in the 1950s in Mornington, Victoria. I'm the youngest of three children, and I have a brother and a sister. Ours was an emotionally dysfunctional household. My father had been a prisoner of the Japanese in World War Two, and he returned home in very poor health, as did they all. Interestingly, he lived till he was nearly ninety-one years old. Dad had told me not long before he passed to spirit that after the war, the returning prisoners were told not to expect to live beyond forty to forty-five years of age.

Fully aware of this miserable prognosis, my poor mother faced a life of raising children alone while expecting that her husband could die at any time. Dad would certainly have had post-traumatic stress disorder, which was not recognised or treated as such at the time. After the war the soldiers were told to just go back and get on with it. I have early recollections of Dad's nightmares – the lasting effects of contracting malaria – and we would all wake up to his screaming in the middle of night. Dad had been assigned to the medical unit as an orderly during the encampment on the Burma–Thai Railway construction, and he was involved with caring for the sick.

I feel that Dad may also have had a strong case of survivor guilt, because my mother's younger brother didn't return from the war, having succumbed to the cruel treatment of prisoners at Sandakan in Borneo. Only six people returned from that island, and her brother died just a few months before the war ended. I believe that these tragic circumstances led my maternal grandmother to join the Spiritualist Church.

My childhood years were difficult ones. We had little money, and there were times when my father wasn't well enough to work or there was simply no work to be found. Dad didn't like my mother working; in his mind that meant he wasn't able to provide for the family. There was always tension in the house, and I have no recollection of my brother living at home. He left home at fourteen and boarded with a local family. Sadly, he suffered our father's anger, frustration and residual war trauma, as he was only three years old when Dad came home.

There was limited interaction in the family home, and though finances were scant, we were always provided for in terms of food, clothing and a roof over our heads, but there was little affection. These were also times of children being seen and not heard. I was always very much the black sheep of the family and was constantly referred to as such by my household and relatives. I was not close to any of them, so I kept to myself. Mornington was a rural area at that time, so I spent a lot of time out of doors sitting in a large oak tree in our backyard. I was an observer of life, because there was nothing really to participate in.

I feel that my perceived 'difference' in the family was in fact the characteristics that offered potential for spirit to work with me, and this difference was something that the family couldn't cope with. Sunday school was attended at the local Methodist church, but I don't have much memory about learning anything from the Bible. I like to think that even at that early age spirit blocked any specific information that might skew my open-mindedness and ultimate mediumship potential. In saying that, I have absolutely no disregard for any religious teaching or practice; it just wasn't for me.

I started my working life in a retail position selling clothes and haberdashery. I later joined the Bank of New South Wales in 1971, and I worked there for sixteen years. I was married in 1977 and left the bank just prior to the birth of our daughter, Natalie. I was fortunate enough to be in a stable marriage at that time, and I was grateful to be able to stay at home for two years taking care of our baby daughter.

I had no idea that I possessed the gift of mediumship until my early fifties, when my life changed significantly. It was in the early 2000s when my interest began, following my marriage breakdown. I started seeking out mediums and psychics for readings, anything that could potentially help me in my state of distress. As my own interest, skills and knowledge increased, I began to understand why my life had been so challenging up to this point.

By 2002 I had become very interested in mediumship and Spiritualism in general, and I started going to the Victorian Spiritualist Union (VSU) for the Sunday service, which was then held at the A'Beckett Street Spiritualist Church in the centre of Melbourne. I developed a real passion for reading anything and everything I could about mediumship.

As a baby I had been christened in the Christian Spiritualist Church at Armadale in Melbourne, and from early childhood I was always told about my christening and the importance of being a Spiritualist, even though it is not a common religion at all in Australia. It wasn't then, and it still isn't to this day. I still have the christening certificate, which indicates that my Spiritualist name is Rosemary, and there were three floral wreaths that were given to me at the time, in accordance with Spiritualist tradition. I knew of these wreaths because my mother had kept them for many years, but sadly she must have thrown them away at some point.

My maternal grandmother was involved with Spiritualism at the time, and I believe she would have been instrumental in my christening being held at her church. I have read that a medium will always recognise the mediumship potential in a baby, and I now believe this is what happened for me. I was the only one in my family to be christened as such, and these days it would be called a 'naming'.

Growing up, nothing was ever discussed about mediumship or the Spiritualist Church, so no information was ever passed on to me. In 2012 I found out through a distant cousin that my late grandmother was a medium; we were at my aunt's funeral at the time, and I was amazed by this news. My paternal grandmother also had an interest in this sphere of life, but again no information was ever passed on. It's really unfortunate that I never knew anymore, but that was the case in those days.

Around 2004 I started attending Spiritualist churches around Melbourne just out of interest. I joined my first development circle around the same time; I only stayed for six months before joining another circle some six months later, where I participated for approximately four years. Development circles can engender either positive or negative energy. Unfortunately, the first circle for me was the latter, a crushing experience that left me absolutely riddled with self-doubt and sapped of all my confidence as a medium.

One would hope and expect that the leader of a mediumship development circle would be supportive and full of encouragement for those who choose to work for spirit, but that is not necessarily the case. I nearly gave up my mediumship altogether, except for the encouragement of a very dear friend, Melanie, who passed to spirit in 2014. I will be forever grateful for Melanie's insistence that I return to it. She had no interest in mediumship herself, but she had some wonderful psychic abilities and could sense the need I had for my mediumship. She continues to make her presence felt in my life, albeit now from the other side.

In 2006 I decided to go to the United Kingdom for an indefinite period; I luckily have dual citizenship, and my daughter was about to turn nineteen, so I knew she could look after herself at home, as well as care for our dogs. The next year I flew off on my adventure, and I believe my entire trip was being guided by spirit; I absolutely trusted that all would be well. I had booked a week-long course at Arthur Findlay College. The course was called 'Introduction to Mediumship', and it was being run by the Reverend Val Williams; it proved to be a remarkable event.

There was a lovely older English woman attending the course. Her name was Violet Du Rose. She had a nervous disorder that restricted her ability at the dining table, and on the first day she asked if I would sit with her at meal-times and help with getting her food and cutting it up, which I was very happy to do. On the final day Violet and I were the only two left in the reception area waiting to leave. Violet went often to Arthur Findlay and had made private arrangements with a taxi company to get her back home. We both decided on a code word that would be used by whoever arrived in the spirit world first, to indicate their presence to the other. Our code word was 'Stansted'. Violet passed to spirit some years later, and when I was attending the Spiritualist church at Mornington, the medium doing the demonstration came to me and her initial words were, 'You went to Stansted, didn't you?' Then followed the most beautiful reading with wonderful evidence that it was Violet communicating with me.

There was no stopping mediumship for me after that amazing experience in the United Kingdom, and I performed my first platform demonstration at the Mornington church soon after arriving home. It was a real honour to be invited. I have now been a member of the VSU since 2004 and a member of the Spiritualists' Union (UK) since 2008.

In 2008 I started sitting in a healing/mediumship development circle with Reverend Bob Ferguson, who had many years of experience and had established the Spiritualist church in Mornington in the late 1970s. Bob and his wife Lisa were very dedicated to Spiritualism, and tragically had lost their only son to an asthma attack when he was in his late teens. I attended the Mornington church on an ongoing basis and did platform there many times. I also often read the healing prayer as part of the regular service, so that Bob could do the healing work. He was a very good healer, and through sitting in his circle for a number of years I accumulated my hours for healing practice to be awarded a certificate in spiritual healing.

My mother passed in 2005 and my father in 2010. I was very aware of my parents' presence around me almost immediately after their deaths, and this helped to temper my sadness. Though I wasn't close to either of my parents throughout my life, I always knew there would be a closeness in our relationship once they both passed. This has proved to be the case, and I have received some truly wonderful readings and messages from mediums, both here and in the United Kingdom, who have connected with my parents in spirit.

I have never worked full-time as a medium. I would have liked to, and I was confident that it would be possible to do so, but my experience proved otherwise; it only ever provided pocket money for me. After a time I began to realise that the readings were more of a healing for some people and the financial side became secondary. Sometimes the readings would last well beyond the allotted time, and I never rushed anyone in leaving.

Ultimately, I became more involved in the philosophy of Spiritualism and was extensively involved with the Mornington Spiritualist Church for a few years and then with the VSU, being a committee member and house medium, who did the platform demonstrations, lectures, healing and one-on-one readings when required. I was a committee member at the VSU from 2011 to 2015 and was vice-president for two years in that time.

From 2010 to 2012 I did mediumship demonstrations at a small cafe called Center Stage in the bayside suburb of Chelsea in Melbourne. They had a small stage area, and each month they would have a Saturday-night dinner with entertainment, including piano recitals, singing, small musical groups and mediumship. It was very successful, and I gained a lot of confidence with my mediumship by participating at these events.

I left the VSU in 2015 after moving away from the city two years earlier to live in the large regional town of Ballarat. I was looking for a quieter, less hectic life, and the travel time and distance to and from Melbourne became too much of a challenge for me in continuing with the VSU. Moving to the country has meant I rarely use my mediumship abilities anymore, which is a shame.

In 2017 I established a Spiritualist church in Ballarat, but the town is very conservative, with a long tradition for the orthodox Christian churches, though long ago there have been Spiritualist churches here in the past. My church was called Ballarat Spiritualist Fellowship, and it survived for two years, from 2017 to 2019. I closed it because there was no regular support in terms of available platform mediums, and the long distance from Melbourne was prohibitive for many to attend on a regular basis. I thought it was unfair to ask the mediums to travel so far and then work on the platform.

The church meetings were held fortnightly, and I would run the service, do the lecture and often also the mediumship demonstration. A healing prayer was always included, as is usual in a Spiritualist church service, but I had no healers either, and there was little interest from the people who came regularly in learning about mediumship themselves. Occasionally, I had friends who would make the one-and-a-half-hour trip from Melbourne to help out on the platform. As much as I loved doing the work for the church, the accompanying organisational aspects required in running it became too much for one person, and I decided to close.

My pursuit of mediumship has changed me in many ways; however, it was my search for relevant philosophical knowledge that led me to a love of reading, not only about Spiritualist philosophy and the whys and hows of mediumship but also about metaphysics, theosophy and general philosophy. I call it self-study, and ultimately I now have a greater understanding of myself and my place in the world.

With mediumship there is always the stress of trying to meet people's expectations. I found that some people have unrealistic ideas about what mediumship is; they almost expect that you can recreate the presence of their loved one or predict their future for them in enormous detail. This is not what mediumship is about. Also, the terms 'medium', 'psychic', 'clairvoyant' and 'Tarot reader' have become interchangeable in the modern-day lexicon, giving the impression of a superficial 'airy-fairy' process that is often dismissed as non-deserving of serious attention.

Personal attacks, scorn, ridicule and general ignorance are so difficult to deal with. I've been publicly criticised by people whether they know me or not and openly compared to others, not realising that every medium is different and has varying skills. Sadly, I found this to be particularly apparent when I was running my church. People often come with preconceived ideas and expectations of who they want messages from, and they assume their expectations will be met by the medium. It's never up to the medium to choose who comes through; it's only ever spirit who decides that!

At one service at my church in Ballarat I was giving a reading to a new member of the congregation. I gave what I call 'good evidence', and I was able to feel the kind energy from their loved one in spirit. The woman blatantly told me I was wrong and was far from the truth. Obviously, I was shocked, as I knew what I was experiencing to be true. I received an email from her a few days later; she had reflected on the reading and realised who was communicating and why. She had assumed it was someone else in spirit at the time, and this is often where the problem lies: the recipients have certain unrealistic expectations about who is communicating with the medium.

As far as friends are concerned, I intentionally distanced myself from some. Not everyone likes what I do, and I have had comments like, 'I don't believe in all that stuff,' or 'So, you call up the dead?' One very religious friend who I have known since we were teenagers joined an extremely orthodox Christian church and told me that she would pray for me. Perhaps a kindly gesture, but it had the feeling of judgement and scorn.

Generally, I don't tell anyone what I'm doing with my mediumship, because it becomes way too difficult to explain. Once I started seriously on the path of mediumship I didn't really attempt to explain what I was doing to any of my family members either. My daughter Natalie is the only family member who knows the detail of what I do. She is extremely supportive and, I think, proud of it. She has mediumship abilities as well, and I share with her as much as I possibly can because I think it's important she has a good foundation of mediumship, should she ever choose to embark on this path.

Religion doesn't play a part in my life; however, I would attend a Spiritualist church if there was a reputable one near me, but sadly there isn't, so location is an issue. I do believe there is an ultimate greater power (God). I also value the Seven Principles of Spiritualism as a 'life code' so to speak, incorporating the notion that there is a God and we are, as human beings, a brotherhood in the broader sense of the term that is not gender specific. I wouldn't choose to attend a Christian church, unless for a wedding or funeral. I believe that mainstream orthodox religions have cast doubt and fear about mediumship for many years, probably since Spiritualism became prominent in the 1800s.

Of all the aspects of mediumship, I love doing platform work most. The energy is always different. I think this is because it's a quick process so the medium is acutely aware of the emotions that are being experienced from the spirit communicator, often ranging from excitement and exhilaration to extreme sadness and sometimes with feelings of guilt and remorse. These are not my feelings, of course; they are the emotions being transmitted from spirit. The upliftment that I feel afterwards can provide a natural high that lasts for many hours.

At this point in time (2020), I see my future work being more involved with healing. I feel that spiritual healing is a way I can help those in need, which is particularly relevant at present due to the distress caused by the chaos of the Covid-19 pandemic. I have established a Distant Spiritual Healing practice for those who ask, and there is no need for personal contact with distant healing, so it's something that can be accessed remotely from anywhere.

In my nearly twenty years of experience there are a couple of one-on-one readings that stand out, each for different reasons. Generally, I don't remember much at all about the readings that I do, the reason being that the messages come from spirit and the medium is the mouthpiece only. I will on occasion remember a few significant details, which I would like to share.

In early 2012 I had noticed an evening news item on the television about a shocking car accident in which three young men had lost their lives and the car had caught on fire. It wasn't at all in my daily routine to watch the news at that time of day, so the circumstances struck me even more. All I could think of was the horror, and I remember saying to myself out loud, 'Those poor families!' Some weeks later an appointment was made for a reading. It was made by a woman called Kerry, and she wanted to bring along her husband, who she didn't name. I never ask for surnames when booking appointments because I always want to keep the reading 'pure', so no-one can suggest I had researched the people in any way.

Kerry and her husband, Sergio, arrived for the sitting, and I remember starting off the reading saying, 'I feel like I have the grief of a mother who has lost a son, aged between eighteen and twenty years', and it went on from there to reveal the loss of their beloved son, Sam, who was nineteen. Kerry and I have kept in contact since that time, and she went on to write her book *A Mother's Journey: a story of everlasting love and evidence of life after death*. It all seems so surreal that I am now sharing my own story in Kerry's next book. I've learnt not to question such things; they are just meant to be.

I have a great fondness for psychic portraiture, and at times I would do a portrait prior to someone coming for a reading. I usually do it the day beforehand and give it to the sitter before we start the reading. Psychic portraiture is where spirit uses my hand to create a portrait of a spirit face. I have limited drawing skills, but I can produce the artwork this way. Prior to a reading, I was preparing the portrait and I just couldn't get one of the eyes right. It was a sketch of an elderly gentleman, and it had been quite an easy and straightforward picture, except for one eye. My experience with previous portraits had been that I just knew when it was complete; there would be no more energy coming through, so I would finish.

In this case I tried to fix the look of one eye and nothing worked, so I decided to stop. The couple who came for the reading were lovely, very gentle, well-dressed and middle-aged. I gave them the portrait, and they said they recognised who it was but didn't tell me the spirit's identity. The man pointed to the portrait and looked at his wife and smiled. I took their reaction to be one of judgement as to the quality or skill of the portrait, pointing out the discrepancy in the eyes. At the end of the reading the man told me that his father had a 'turned eye', and I had captured it perfectly. Thank you, spirit!

Personally, I'm not at all afraid to die; however, I don't want to be in pain or suffering long-term decline or illness. I believe people have a right to choose to die, so I am a supporter of assisted dying. I see death as a rebirth into a great pool of soul energy, where we recognise our loved ones who have already passed, by their energy. It's important to have an open mind and a broad view of death being a part of life.

I would like to share some observations I have made along the way that may be of benefit to aspiring mediums.

Self-care: The emotional, spiritual and physical energy required to be a medium can be exhausting. There is a need to be aware that dealing with other people's trauma and sadness can have a serious and potentially long-term effect called compassion fatigue, so it's important not to sacrifice one's own wellbeing. Just because you have this gift doesn't mean you are always accessible to people or to spirit. Your work for spirit must fit in with the schedule of your daily life.

An observation: If you are committed to your mediumship and are willing to work with and for spirit, you will be supported by them. Trust in the leadership and strength of the spirit guides who work with you and know and understand that mediumship is never about you; it's about being of service to spirit.

Remember that all mediums will have a different skill set. Don't compare yourself to others. Your skills are unique because your life will have been different to everyone else's. Spirit will use your skills to their advantage, and thus you will have a valuable contribution to make. It's not about being able to display a percentage of accuracy, which seems to be a common and misguided yardstick; the value of your work can only be measured by your ability to touch the soul of everyone who comes to you for a reading.

Overwhelmingly, my work with mediumship has given me such pleasure and joy, not only because I have recognised and understood my personal growth but also because I was able to witness the help and healing that was brought to people in often very tragic and distressing circumstances.

Medium and healer
Age: in 60s
Ballarat, Australia

lculross@gmail.com

Chapter nine

SIMONE SALMON

In 2019, I met Simone at Arthur Findlay College, where we shared the same dining table for all three daily meals over the week. Right from the outset I found Simone to be warm, funny and very engaging. Simone is loud and passionate about all that she does, and it's easy to be swept up in her genuine enthusiasm. At the college we both discussed our writing, among many other things, and Simone has written her own book, called *Drafnel*, which was published a few years ago in the United States. A late starter to mediumship like myself, I was very keen to learn what sent Simone on her mediumistic pathway. Simone is Jamaican born and lives in New York.

I was born in Jamaica in the West Indies, and I grew up in the city of Harbor View in Kingston 17. As an eleven-year-old, I emigrated to the United States with my younger three siblings, two brothers and a sister. We are all just one year apart in age. Prior to moving to the States, my siblings, a female cousin and I all lived with our paternal grandmother, who raised us.

My mother had me when she was just sixteen years old, and her other three children followed not long afterwards in quick succession. My father was also very young when I was born, and when he turned twenty-two years old he left his young family behind in Jamaica to go to college in the United States to study accounting.

My mother didn't finish high school, and she never liked talking about her past with me or with anyone else. Originally, my siblings and I lived with both our parents in Harbor View, but after my father had been gone for about a year, my mother packed up and followed him to live in the Bronx in New York, where Dad was studying. After arriving in New York my mother went to a secretarial school to train in becoming a secretary. Us children all stayed behind in Jamaica to live with my cousin and grandmother, and that was how we were raised.

In Jamaica I spent a lot of my time in the Church of God, where there was lots of singing and clapping, just like in the Gospel churches in the USA. Church was a place where we went regularly. Our grandmother was very devout, and she gave us no other choice but to go along with her. We were young, and there was nothing else for us to do. Fortunately for me I loved going to church, and I went almost every day. My grandmother was very strict, so going to church was one of the very few social outlets that we had, and for all of us kids church was a way to escape the confines of the house. When we weren't in school, our weekdays consisted of Youth Ministry, and on the weekends, you guessed it, we all attended church!

My great-grandmother, who was Grandma's mum, lived in the country, and when I was around six years old she came and stayed with us for what seemed like ages. I loved my great-grandmother very much; she was hilarious and always a lot of fun to be around. I wasn't aware of the circumstances at the time as to why she came to stay; I can only assume that she wasn't well. Sadly, while she was living with us, she passed away in our home. Later, my cousin and I used to sleep in the same room that my great-grandmother had died in, and I still vividly remember that I could feel my great-grandmother's spiritual presence in the room. This wasn't a feeling of comfort to me as a six-year-old child; I was terrified. I felt genuine fear when I had to sleep in the room, because I knew that somehow this unseen presence was in there too.

Every year from the age of four to eleven years, my two brothers, my sister and I were all flown to the United States during the summer school holidays, so we could visit and stay with our parents in New York. We all loved these trips, and they offered us some much-needed variety to our constant diet of school and church back in Jamaica. On one trip my mother asked me if I wanted to go back to live with my grandmother, and I said no. So the decision was made, and we all stayed in the Bronx to live with our parents.

My early years of primary school and my first year of high school were all spent in Jamaica, where the school system is much more advanced than in the United States. I started attending high school in the Bronx near to where we lived. I worked hard at my studies, and I was a good student. At fourteen, while I was still at high school, I took a part-time job after school working in retail so that I could make some extra money to buy my own clothes. Even though my father was working as an accountant and my mother was a secretary, it was hard for my parents to make enough money to house, clothe and feed all six of us. While I was completing high school my parents decided to separate, and they later divorced when I was at college. I still see them both, and they have managed to move on with their lives. Both have remarried, but sadly my mother has since been widowed.

After I finished high school I went to college in Manhattan, New York, to study computer science. Just as I had secretly foreseen, I got an internship in my junior year at college with International Business Machines (IBM). When I was around seven or eight years old, I had a natural ability to make things happen, and I could manifest certain situations at will. I would mentally plant the seed about what I wanted to come true, and it always became my reality. Some things took longer than others to happen, but they always did come to fruition eventually. I knew that one day I would work for IBM. I had set that very intention, and that's what happened for me. I've continued to manifest positive outcomes and real situations throughout my life ever since.

As I got older another ability became apparent to me: I had become very psychic. At the time I had no real concept of what being psychic meant, but I would just know in advance what was about to happen. These were simple things, but they were a real constant in my life and they came very naturally to me. I would know when the telephone was about to ring and who would be calling. I knew when the doorbell was about to sound and who would be standing on the other side of the door. These psychic experiences didn't happen just once or twice, they became a part of my daily life, and I really enjoyed being able to do this.

After I had graduated from college, I was renting an apartment in a beautiful old brownstone house in Brooklyn, New York, with my friend Tracey. In this apartment I would continually hear young children running up and down inside the building, but I also knew that no children lived there or in the co-adjoined building next door. I had no idea where these unseen voices were coming from. One day I was in the kitchen. It was just on dusk, and as I looked outside the window I saw a woman dressed in white drifting past outside. I did a double take, but she was no longer there. When I turned around, the woman in white was now inside our apartment going up the stairs to the bedrooms. I tried to make some sense of what I was seeing, so I started to think logically and decided that it had to be Tracey. Tracey was out at the time, but I couldn't comprehend what I saw, and I was looking for all types of feasible answers. I called Tracey's name and she didn't answer, so I went upstairs to her room, but she wasn't there and neither was the woman in white.

I don't know if I believed in the afterlife back then. I knew within myself that spirits existed, and I had always believed that the human soul survived a physical death, but I couldn't explain what I had just witnessed. While living in this old brownstone house I constantly heard my name being called. I could never see anyone, but I could certainly hear them. I still didn't attach the name mediumship to what was happening to me. I knew from my previous experiences of sensing my great-grandmother's spirit that I had a natural ability to connect with people who had passed, but I didn't understand this as being mediumship.

I guess my life just took over then, and I did the normal things people do as they make their way through. I started working in the corporate world in the financial sector with various large companies, and I did this on and off over a period of many years. I met a man and had two sons to him, who I raised alone after he left just before my youngest son was born. I've always been fiercely independent and continued to work and raise my young family alone. A business opportunity arose, and I decided to leave my corporate role to try something new. I bought and ran a franchise business of my own in commercial cleaning, and I did this for five years. After working for myself I realised that self-employment was quite stressful on many levels, so I decided to go back to the business world where I worked managing word processing, printing and copying centres.

I was still no closer to discovering what being psychic really meant, but I kept hearing the term 'psychic'. I had experienced a lifetime of 'knowing' myself, and I felt that finally the time had come to explore things properly for myself. I started doing a lot of reading and online study to learn more about the world of psychic sciences, and I was totally fascinated by what I learnt. My research took me down a virtual rabbit hole to gain as much information as I possibly could about these so-called psychics. I desperately needed to know if psychic episodes were real or just made up.

In 2013 my own journey began when I had an overwhelming need to discover the existence of miracles. I began doing daily meditations, and this was quite new to me. However, I could meditate very easily simply by playing a guided meditation on my phone, and away I would go. One day I was listening to a meditation by the American motivational speaker Esther Hicks when I felt a huge surge of electricity rush up and down the entire length of my body. I had never experienced energy that powerful before, and I was in a state of bliss. That was my turning point, and from then on I wanted to learn more about what had caused that amazing energy current and if it was related in some way to miracles.

I decided to create my own online event called the MiracleMindFest Teleseminar, which was all about helping those involved to create their own miracles. At the event I wanted to discuss all types of psychic phenomena, including mediumship, but I didn't know how I was going to make this happen. To start the process I instinctively set the intention of what I wanted to achieve. I said to myself that if this is all real, then I will be able to manifest this event to make it become a reality.

I decided to personally reach out to speakers from other online seminars I had attended, and before I knew it I booked psychics and mediums one by one until I had twenty-one contributors who all wanted to be a part of what I was doing. These mediums and psychics were all well established and widely known in their fields, and they all wanted to be involved in teaching other curious participants about what they did in their work.

Creating the conference from nothing was a miracle in itself, but I wanted to show people that miracles were possible and they happen all the time. I felt that people needed to know that if they opened their minds up to the small miracles each day, these in turn would allow them to see the larger miracles of life, such as their own psychic and mediumistic gifts. It was through this online conference that I began to explore my own psychic abilities as well, and I discovered the MontClair Psychic School in New Jersey, where I took numerous classes to help develop my psychic abilities further.

The accelerated psychic development classes at the MontClair Psychic School were run by a wonderful teacher and psychic medium called Lee VanZyl, who is originally from South Africa. Lee's classes were not like a spiritual circle; these were more of a class situation where the students were there to specifically learn about their abilities and how they could use them. The way we developed our abilities was not so much a gentle unfoldment, as you might expect in a spiritual development group; these were classes that were designed to push you along quite quickly. They worked for me, and I can honestly say that these were some of the best lessons I have ever experienced and where I mostly learnt how to hone my own abilities.

I've always been what I call a 'seeker', and I seek the truth in all that I do. I want to know how things happen and how they come to be. It's important to try to find the truth behind the truth, and for me everything is experiential; you need to experience something in order to actually believe that it's true. Because of my beliefs, I was unable and unwilling to just be told that mediumship existed and that it was real. I had to experience mediumship for myself before I could really believe in it.

After taking numerous classes and developing my psychic abilities more, I was able to join Lee's mediumship development circle, which she also ran from the same location in New Jersey. I needed the whole concept of mediumship to be demystified for myself, because in Jamaican culture it is considered taboo to talk to the dead. I was initially scared to death to start the mediumship classes because I thought I was going to see ghosts. I really had no idea what to expect.

Before starting any of the mediumship courses I had randomly been looking online and saw a photograph of a beautiful mansion called the Arthur Findlay College (AFC). I immediately thought that I really wanted to take classes there too. After reading the article under the photo, I realised that this college was in England, so for me this was out of the question. It was just another dream to add to my bucket list. Once I started attending my mediumship development circle with Lee, I began to meet other new people, and many of them had been to AFC to study. They all seemed to love their experience there, so I became even more curious.

I was forty-eight years old when Lee first started to teach me about mediumship. Lee talked about the importance of sharing as much evidence as possible to show the spirit communicator's survival into the spirit world. Lee also explained to us that at the end of a reading there is likely to be a special message that often tends to be words of love that offer comfort to the recipient. I later learnt that good mediumship can't just be about the message alone, because messages aren't actual evidence of the survival of the soul into the spirit world, as they can't be validated. Sometimes the real message will be all wrapped up in the evidence of what is shared during the reading, and nothing more is needed at the end. Lee was a wonderful teacher, and she taught me much.

In 2015 I wrote a book called *Drafnel*, which is loosely based on my personal story. In the book I wrote about my psychic and mediumship abilities and some experiences I have had. Because I'm not fully 'out of the closet' with my mediumship, I decided to write the book as a fictional novel and not as a biography. Doing so enabled me to turn a small part of my unusual reality into a paranormal fantasy story, and I felt more comfortable in writing my story that way.

Throughout my life I have always been gainfully employed, and I have never had any issues in finding good jobs that have allowed me to live comfortably and to support my two sons. In early 2016 I decided I wanted to work full-time as a medium, so I had to resign from my corporate job. I wanted to do online readings only, to eliminate the need for people coming into my home, but this business model didn't take off and I admit that I was quite naive in how I went about marketing myself as a medium. With the lack of ongoing readings and my mediumship being my sole source of income this was unsustainable and, after a year, I had no choice but to start working again in mainstream employment. My mediumship readings continued, but as a secondary sideline.

In 2019 the opportunity arose when I too could go to the United Kingdom to do a one-week course at AFC. It was like a dream come true, and I had the most amazing time at the college, followed by a short holiday in Paris for a week, where my two adult sons flew over to be with me. I absolutely loved my time studying all aspects of mediumship, and I can't wait to return in the future.

My tutor was Simone Key, and I was drawn to her from the first time I searched the college's website. We both share a first name, and her last name is very similar to my sons', so it felt very right to be with her; and it was. During my week I managed to overcome the stage fright that would normally overcome me each time I do a platform demonstration. Stage fright is common with many students starting out, and one of my primary goals was to come away from the college feeling more comfortable when demonstrating, and I did manage to achieve that.

Even though I am now in my mid-fifties, only my two sons, my niece and a few close friends know that I am a medium. Everyone has been extremely supportive of me, and no-one has expressed any issues at all about what I do. The paradox is that my extended family would look down at me if they knew I was a medium, yet I'm aware that many of them have sought guidance from people who practice Obeah, which is a type of Hoodoo practised in Jamaica. In Jamaica it is widely regarded as forbidden to communicate with the dead, and I know that my family think that mediums are not normal people and they ignorantly believe that mediums are evil and work with the devil. I'm acutely aware they are unlikely to be supportive of me, so I prefer to say nothing about my mediumship with them.

My family history is an interesting one. My maternal grandmother was unofficially adopted by a Jamaican family. Her birth family was originally from India, and my grandmother had a twin brother, who apparently died as a child. My grandmother's family gave her away to a Jamaican family to be their unpaid 'helper', which was quite common back then. Sadly, this happened to many children who came from large families, in which their parents couldn't afford to care for them. The child would be given away and raised elsewhere, in return for their board and keep.

One of my grandmother's 'adopted sisters' was known to me as Aunt C, and she was a psychic, who also read tea leaves. Family members on my mother's side would go to Aunt C for readings, and when I was little I never wanted to go near her because I was so afraid of this weird practice of reading futures in tea leaves. Of course, I didn't really understand any of it, but I was still frightened for some reason. Once my mother went to Aunt C to have a spell created to protect my brother from evil spirits, which was apparently another one of her talents.

In 2019 I started a podcast called *Messages from the Other Side*. I interview a whole range of people, whether they be psychics, mediums or just individuals with stories to share about paranormal activities. It was important for me to create a platform where people could contribute their own stories and experiences. Mostly this became my main outlet to feel safe in sharing my abilities with an audience interested in learning more about the supernatural. The platform also allowed me to quietly build a personal presence, without the pressure of hard selling my services to strangers, which I'm not comfortable in doing.

Later that year I lost my younger sister to breast cancer. She was still so young and had just turned fifty when she passed. We were not very close, and I hadn't shared my mediumship abilities with her or the amount of study I'd been doing over the years to develop as a medium. She was aware I had done some healing work with Lee VanZyl, but I know she didn't understand what that really entailed. As she became sicker with the cancer, I asked her if I could do some healing for her, but she didn't seem interested and I certainly didn't want to push the subject. We were together when she passed, just the two of us. I witnessed Archangel Michael come to help her pass over and into the light, which was truly beautiful to witness. Since then she has been in my dreams often, and she has shared information with me that has been very important in my life. I know that these dreams are actual visits from her. I find them very comforting. and I always try to listen carefully to what she tells me from the other side.

As much as I loved going to church as a young girl in Jamaica, I no longer feel that way now. I do still believe in God, but that is where my religious beliefs start and end. I feel that the main purpose of religion is to control the masses, and that's something I cannot spiritually reconcile with. I choose to believe there is a higher consciousness that is responsible for all there is and for all that can be. I also feel that many religions have taught people to believe that the natural abilities of mediums are somehow evil and unnatural. Most religions refuse to recognise or understand the medium's gift to communicate with the dead, and they label mediums as unholy and ungodly. For those mediums who recognise their abilities early on, they are taught to suppress those gifts or deny themselves completely, so they can be considered normal by the church; I can't stand for that.

I'm currently working full-time in a new business I have created, providing business consulting for various agencies and corporations. Once my finances have hit the intended goal, I plan on devoting time again to my mediumship, but for now I'm putting my mediumship completely on hold. My podcast is also being set aside, as is the writing of any new books, but these holds are only temporary. This doesn't mean I am no longer a medium; once a medium, always a medium. It simply means that I've made a conscious choice right now not to do any readings for clients or to do any further study with my mediumship. My abilities will always exist. They won't disappear, and I look forward to reading for people again when I feel ready to do so.

Mediumship is a truly beautiful way to help those who are grieving and in need of healing. We are the link that brings the two worlds together, and knowing that I can do that is more than enough for me.

Queens, New York, United States of America
Age, 56
Entrepreneur, author and medium

www.simonesalmon.com
info@simonesalmon.com

Chapter ten

FLORENCE KING

Florence is well known in her native Sydney as a platform medium and she also teaches mediumship to her many students, primarily in Sydney's western suburbs. I first knew of Florence through my childhood friend Sandra Uzowuru, who I went to Arthur Findlay College with in 2015. Sandra had been studying mediumship with Florence, which gave her a good grounding and readiness to attend the college. Florence is a regular guest speaker and facilitator at many of the Mind, Body and Spirit Festivals and other similar events in Australia. We met in person for the first time in October 2019 at the Mind, Body and Spirit Festival in Sydney, where we both ran seminars. There is a genuine Aussie warmth about Florence, which I liked immediately. Florence has also written and published a number of books herself about mediumship.

I'm an only child born in Waterloo, Sydney, and I was raised in Smithfield, some thirty kilometres from the Sydney CBD. We were a working-class family with an abundance of love, but not a lot of money. My mother, Edna, was previously a machinist, and she stayed home to raise me while my father, Tony, worked as a sheet metal worker and supported the family financially. My parents were always very present in my life and in all that I did. They were both hard workers, and they passed this strong work ethic on to me.

Growing up I hated school and couldn't wait to leave, so at fifteen, I did. The problem with leaving school early was that I didn't have any real qualifications to find a decent job. Being tall and slender when I was young led to comments that I should do modelling work, so aged sixteen I did a modelling course with the well-known and highly respected June Dally-Watkins. My first modelling job was doing a swimsuit shoot to begin my portfolio, and I soon decided that it wasn't for me – my very brief modelling career came to an abrupt end.

Throughout my lifetime I've had a huge range of jobs, primarily in retail, which suited my genuine love of people.

My family believed in God and, oddly, we all had an interest in mediums and psychics, but none of us understood much about what they really did or what the difference was between the two. I had always presumed they were one and the same, just with two different names. Every now and then we all went together to see psychics to have readings done. I guess we were naively looking for something amazing to happen at these sittings, and we were expecting some sort of communication with the spirit world; however, we weren't aware that only mediums can do that and not psychics. I'm not sure how or why my parents had this enthusiasm for the paranormal, but they did, and it fascinated me too.

I lost a cousin who was like a sister to me. She died at twenty-seven with a brain tumour. Her passing affected me greatly and then, unbelievably, my fiancé was killed instantly in a car accident, when his car collided with a pole due to high speed. I had no warning; it wasn't like he had an illness, so I wasn't remotely prepared for losing him. His short life was over in a second. He was only twenty-five years old; I was twenty-six, and together we had a nineteen-month-old son. Having a young baby with no memories of his father was a very cruel blow. My fiancé was buried a week before Christmas, and my life was forever changed.

Years later I met and married my husband, Bruce, and we went on to have three more wonderful children. This happiness temporarily ended when both of my parents passed away within eleven weeks of each other; both had cancer. I was four months pregnant with my fourth child when Mum was first diagnosed, and she was given twelve months to live, but tragically she died after only four. My mum passed at home, and I was so grateful to be able to care for her during that time. I was eight months pregnant when I lost her, and then my dad started to slip away as well. To watch his decline and to eventually lose him too eleven weeks later was beyond surreal, and it was a truly devastating time for me and my family.

Four years after my parents' passing, an opportunity presented itself for me to attend a spiritual development class, and I was immediately drawn to doing this. Over the years I had sadly miscarried seven babies, and I really wanted to learn more about the afterlife and I hoped that these classes would help answer my questions. I was forty-four years old when the first class began, and my main priority was to see if I could make a connection with one of my own loved ones in spirit. Unbelievably, my ability to connect with the spirit world happened almost instantly.

The sensation of communicating with spirit felt like I had somehow found my place in life, and I knew I was destined to do this type of work. I never saw spirit clearly clairvoyantly, but the 'feeling' and the 'knowing' that they were there was clear, and the evidence was fast flowing. I absolutely trusted where I was going, even though I didn't know exactly how far I would go, or where I would end up.

In my classes I was like a sponge soaking up all that was taught to me, and I did a lot of self-study as well, reading as much as I could about mediumship. Within a year, I began working as a medium doing private sittings from our home. None of this was planned; it all just happened, and it astounded my family and me. I would do my readings over several days each week, and I loved helping people in this way. I had found what I had been silently and unknowingly searching for.

I was very happy working with my clients on a one-to-one basis, and I continued to do this. At the same time I had started to attend platform demonstrations at various locations in and around Sydney, and I hungered to do that type of mediumship work too, but I didn't know if I could. I really enjoyed watching the other mediums work, and I became quite addicted to the wonder of it, loving how spirit could work with the mediums in this way.

In order to attract more clients, I began to do home parties for those interested in mediumship, and it was at these evenings that I began doing my first platform demonstrations. At first I wasn't sure how the readings would go, but the responses from the small audiences were always favourable, and I quickly found that I loved working that way with my mediumship.

As an extension of my work, I began attending various Spiritualist churches in Sydney suburbs, and I became one of the platform mediums, which I really enjoyed doing. As my confidence grew in working this way, I began doing platform demonstrations at the Mind Body Spirit Festivals that were held in Sydney and other larger towns and major cities. At the same time I continued doing my private readings from home and at psychic fairs and other charity events.

I became very driven with my mediumship. I would do as many readings as possible each week, and I said yes to every opportunity to work on the platform. My clientele grew massively, and it was all still done through word of mouth, as Facebook and other social media didn't exist back then. It got to the stage where I had a six-month waiting list for private readings and a three-year waiting list for home parties. All truly amazing.

By nature I have always been a compassionate and caring person, and my mediumship has shown me much about other people's lives and their personal suffering. Knowing that I am a medium has deepened my faith in God and in the spirit world; I now look at everything with very different eyes. The hardest thing to witness as a medium is the raw grief you experience from your sitters and knowing there is no quick fix for their pain.

It breaks my heart to witness suffering, and I often cry in private sittings and sometimes even on stage during a demonstration. I've been widely criticised for this 'lack of professionalism', but I will never censor how I feel about people, due to the hardships they've had to endure. The tragedies of others do touch my own heart, and all mediums are deeply sensitive people. It's an absolute requirement in order to do this kind of work. What surprises me most is that these negative comments have come mainly from other psychics and mediums.

Being a medium can make you quite misunderstood by the public as a whole and by friends and family members. I've been incredibly lucky with the wonderful belief, encouragement and support I've received from my own family, but I'm aware this is not always the case for many mediums. My children have always attended the psychic fairs and the Mind Body Spirit Festivals with me; they've grown up with my mediumship. They assist me by taking the bookings for my one-on-one readings at the events, which allows me to spend more time doing actual readings, rather than dealing with enquiries.

With mediumship and psychic work, sceptics are a huge part of the journey, and I feel that this is both understandable and reasonable. There are a lot of frauds in this industry, and sadly there is no real way to police what unscrupulous people do. We must just continue to serve spirit and be the best version of ourselves and not overly stress about what we can't change. I never seek to actively convert anyone into believing in mediumship, but when a spirit communicates with me during a reading, I hope that the standard of my work shows that there is another life beyond this one. For me, this is all I have ever set out to do.

Religion is important to me, but I don't go to church as often as I should; however, I absolutely do believe in God. I was over the moon when a Catholic priest once rang me asking for a reading. I felt like I was getting a direct message of approval from above. The priest ended the phone call by telling me to 'keep up my good work'. Many people have said I am not a good Catholic because of the work I do, but I firmly believe this is what God intended for me, because my mediumship unfoldment happened so easily. How can it be wrong to help people to cope with their grief and to empower them to continue living a worthwhile existence? I feel very at ease with my religious choices, and I attend Spiritual churches as well as the Catholic ones.

It saddens me to see negativity relating to mediumship and psychic readings, and I feel that much of this stems from a lack of education. I believe that too many people working in this field who call themselves psychics and/or mediums do not understand the difference between a medium and a psychic. When a grieving person wants to connect with a loved one in spirit they sometimes inadvertently see a psychic, when in reality they needed to see a medium. This understandably leaves them feeling that they have been taken advantage of; psychics read living energy only, and they don't work with spirit. When any bookings are made, it should be made clear by the psychic and/or medium what services are being offered, and the prospective sitter can then make an informed decision based on their needs.

Death, like birth, is a reality of life, yet most people avoid touching on the subject of their own mortality; talking about death frightens them, and the subject is quite daunting and often taboo. The fear of the unknown is what unnerves people most, and I feel that if we can alleviate the anguish that surrounds a passing, then it will go a long way towards reducing the fear associated with a physical death. A positive mediumship experience can, and will, help to heal grief-stricken loved ones, and knowing that the communication between both worlds can never be severed is life changing.

I have always waited for the right teacher to come along, but so far that hasn't happened for me. My spirit guides have become my teachers, and I feel that I have advanced because of my experiences and connections with these guides. If I could choose a teacher, John

Edward from the United States is someone I would love to train with, as I really admire him and the way he works. I was fortunate to meet John on one of his many visits to Australia. He is humble and knows his craft better than anyone I've seen. He has wonderful charisma and a gentle energy that makes you gravitate to him.

With my platform demonstrations, the biggest audience I have worked with was five hundred people at a charity event, and I love pushing and challenging myself to find the correct recipient in a crowd that big. The daunting part is that everyone is watching and waiting for you connect the spirit communicator to the right receiver, and when this happens, it's great for my confidence as a platform medium.

I've been on live television for more than eight years, and this experience has been a wonderful and unexpected addition to my normal mediumship work. Television has a huge reach, allowing many people all at once to be better educated about what mediums do. I was the longest-serving medium on the *Psychic TV* channel and sometimes I hosted the program, which was a terrific experience. The show ran for eight years, and I was on for six and a half of these. Normalising mediumship has always been important to me, and through my media invitations, I feel I have been able to do this to a degree. I'm also very aware of not wanting to trivialise mediumship or make it look like a 'sideshow' on television. That's not what I'm there for.

I was later selected for a television documentary called *Psychics in the Suburbs*, after being initially approached by the show's producer. The camera crew followed me around for three years, collecting footage from live stage shows and events. The show first screened on the ABC in November 2016, and it has been replayed several times since, and I'm very proud of this achievement. Over the years I've written five books about mediumship, and these publications are all designed to educate aspiring mediums about what to expect when identifying signs from spirit for themselves.

The different dynamics of people can be really interesting. I've had many students join my development classes, and after very little training they ask me to get them on television, radio or on stage to demonstrate. What I notice as a teacher is that too many students want to cut corners and are not prepared to work hard to fine-tune their mediumship abilities. I find this extremely disappointing and disrespectful to the spirit world and also to those mediums who work hard and do the right thing by their clients.

I have lost friends along the way who don't seem to understand what I do as a medium, or why I choose to do it. I've made peace with that, and I don't dwell on their reasons for ending our friendship. We all make our own choices, and I have made mine. To be told by a complete stranger that I've made a difference to their day or I have made them smile or laugh is very important to me, and that is what I truly value. The feedback from my books has been so heartwarming, and when a confirmed sceptic changes their mind about mediumship, this is beyond beautiful.

One platform reading was particularly poignant for me. A male spirit communicator came through to forgive a woman in the audience for her accidental part in his death in a motor vehicle accident. The woman who I was reading for was apparently the driver involved in the fatality that killed the spirit in question. She broke down and cried when I shared his message of forgiveness. After the demonstration was over the woman came up to me and said she felt a wonderful release from within to finally be forgiven for her actions.

Phone readings are often incredible and quite different, as you can only hear a voice on the other end, and you can't see who you are talking to. In one particular phone reading, I had connected with my client's father in spirit, and I remember telling the woman 'to be careful of the sugar', as this was what I received via her dad. I was expecting her to tell me she was a diabetic, and I was floored when she told me that she had just spilled sugar all down her top, as she made a coffee with one hand while holding onto the phone with the other hand. She said it was unbelievable, and it gave her so much happiness to know that in that instant, her father was watching her.

When someone chooses to end their own life the readings are always especially tough because the loved ones left behind have so many unanswered questions. The one thing I constantly hear is, 'Didn't they know how much they were loved?' Guilt often consumes those close to the person who suicided, and all seem to wonder what they may have missed. Could they have changed things and prevented it from happening? During these types of readings we can sometimes provide further information for the grieving loved ones, and some of the blanks can be filled in. There are times when the spirit communicator may convey what they couldn't say when living. This may help, but deaths through suicide come with their own additional layers of adversity. In my experience spirits who have suicided always come through with some levels of regret, as their actions have caused a lot of pain for those who are left behind.

Prior to discovering my mediumship the uncertainty of knowing if there was another life after this one was quite terrifying for me. Now of course I do know that we live on, and my work as a medium has provided me with plenty of evidence that we will all be okay on the other side. Most importantly for me is the realisation that I will meet up with all of my loved ones who I have lost along the way. I find that to be of immense comfort.

My Catholic faith told me there was an eternal paradise, but I wasn't sure in what form this would be. I had so many questions, and initially I was scared of how I would die and what if we stopped being who we fundamentally are as people. What if there was no way to really live again? What if we didn't meet up with our loved ones, because once we got there they had already reincarnated and we were left alone? Through my mediumship work I know that none of these concerns eventuate, and I find that to be extremely comforting. For now, I'm certainly not ready or wanting to leave my living family.

I always trust that spirit knows best, and whatever I'm meant to do in life will be presented clearly to me; it has always been that way. I've been very lucky to travel extensively in Australia with my work, and often my family have been able to travel with me. Much of my teaching work comes through invitations, and over the years I've taught and demonstrated in Victoria, South Australia, Queensland, New South Wales and Canberra in the Australian Capital Territory. So far New Zealand has been my only international trip for work, and I was fortunate to be able to take my daughter along to assist at the three platform demonstrations I performed there.

It is my hope that people will become more educated about the positive aspects of a mediumship reading and to know that the soul is unbreakable. I wish to continue bringing comfort, hope and peace to all those people who grieve their loved ones.

Medium and author
Age, 58
Sydney, Australia

www.florencemedium.com
florencemedium@yahoo.com.au

Chapter eleven

ANDREW MANSHIP

Andrew has been my tutor on two occasions now at Arthur Findlay, and from my first encounter I was immediately impressed by his humour, kindness and compassionate approach to teaching mediumship. Like all of my contributors, I knew nothing more about Andrew and how his mediumship abilities became apparent to him. What I did know was that Andrew still held down a very demanding career as a full-time professional firefighter and taught at the college on his weeks off. This fascinated me, and I wanted very much for Andrew to share how these two very different professions are possible to manage. Andrew is Welsh born and lives in the United Kingdom.

In hindsight, mediumship was absolutely innate within me. As a four-year-old I sensed things in my bedroom, but I didn't have any real understanding about what was happening or what these 'things' were. I have vivid memories of a physical presence being there, and in order to make this reality less frightening I would create all sorts of imagery in my mind, changing these things to look like fairytale characters, and this made me feel safer. My parents didn't really understand what was happening with me and put it all down to my overactive imagination.

The unexplainable experiences I was having were real, but I wasn't taken seriously by the very people who I needed emotional support from, my parents. When you first start to develop your abilities as a medium, you often start to question if what you are receiving is real or not, because it's very surreal to explain. Even now, when it comes to the development of my own mediumship, I feel I'm still dealing with many old issues, and much of this stems from my childhood and not being understood.

My first school was a Catholic convent in Newport in South Wales, where we lived. I was four at the time, and it was while I was still experiencing the presence of spirit people in my bedroom. I went to this horrible place for just one year, and I have strong memories and mental images of the nuns and the Mother Superior. I really can't recall any specific details about what I said or did, but my parents were called to the school by the Mother Superior, and I was denounced as a 'devil-child' by her.

This part of my life is a bit hazy, as I truly shut myself off from the outside world and retreated to the safety of my inner self, my imagination and the realms of the spirit world. I was truly misunderstood after being labelled a devil-child, and this caused great upset for myself and my parents; I became quite unruly for a while at home during this period.

My parents seemed to fear talking with me about the images I was seeing and the experiences I was having, so it wasn't something I could share at all with my family. They had very strong views on such things, and being called a devil-child didn't help my cause either. My father came from a very strong Catholic upbringing, and he wasn't particularly approachable when it came to me trying to share the unusual experiences I was having.

Both of my parents, Lesley and Michael, were in the police force when I was younger, and my maternal grandfather was an inspector in the South Wales police force, which we are all very proud of. When my parents started having their own family, it was understandably difficult to both juggle shift work, so they resigned from the police force and my younger brother, Steven, and I moved home to Aberystwyth on the west coast of Wales, where they took over the running of a pub.

I started attending an incredible primary school called Plascrug, and I was very happy at the lack of nuns. I was told by the teachers that I had a very vivid imagination, and this led me to believe that everything I experienced was all make-believe. Aged six, I started walking to school by myself, and during that time I always sensed that I had people and animals walking along with me; this gave me a lot of comfort and a very powerful feeling. My imagination gave me images of dragons and tigers, and I when I arrived at school I would tell my friends what I was seeing. They all thought that this sounded quite cool. My position of 'coolness' didn't last as we all got older.

I was still a very sensitive person, and I was very aware of this, so once I started high school I made a conscious decision to purposely shut down everything I had been experiencing since early childhood. I really wanted to make a fresh start in my secondary school, and I was prepared to do whatever it took to gain acceptance and to make new friends. After I made this decision I put on a bit of a macho front at school, as I thought I needed to toughen up a bit and be a real man; I was twelve years old at the time.

School was something that never sat well with me from an academic perspective, and as a result I didn't do at all well in my A Levels. I was in freefall by then, and my next option was to attend a further education college; I didn't do well there either academically. When I was nineteen, I barely scraped through a clearing process to get a place at a college in Southampton in England. This meant moving to Southampton by myself to do a two-year Higher National Diploma course in public administration.

Southampton was certainly different to my life in Wales, and I ended up living in the red-light district, surrounded by violence. Just being there was very stressful. The students living in this part of town were constantly being beaten up by the local population, and it was an area of extreme poverty, but moving wasn't really an economic option either. To earn some extra cash while studying, I started working behind the bar in a nightclub and, not surprisingly, I ended up spending more time at the nightclub than I did at college, and halfway through my second year I stopped attending classes and dropped out completely. At the time I was totally running away from myself and from my own sensitivity. I started drinking regularly and taking amphetamines, and that was my way of escaping from everything.

At the end of the two years I had to decide what to do. I didn't graduate because I hadn't finished my diploma, and my parents still had no idea that I had dropped out of college and was working at a nightclub. I really didn't want to go back home to Wales to live. On one hand I had a great relationship with my parents and I could tell them anything at all, but at the same time I felt ashamed of my sense of personal failure, so I chose to say nothing at all.

I was promoted from barman to assistant manager at the nightclub, and a year later I became the manager. I was constantly surrounded by aggression, violence, drugs, alcohol and many other negative forces, and this made me face many of my own demons, so I cleaned up my act and went teetotal for about ten months. The realisation soon came that you only belong in this environment if you are partaking in all of its sordid activities, and I didn't want to do any of that any longer. But for now I was stuck there.

A change was needed, and I started playing rugby again, going to the gym and doing the healthy things I used to do as a teenager, and it felt good. During this time my sensitivity began to creep back in slowly, and I started to care about people again and to sense their needs. I seemed to know what people were about to say before they said it, and at last I was more in tune with myself and the world again.

I began to experience how my own energy could influence my surroundings and all the people in it. If I was in a bad mood at work, everything would go badly, and I soon realised that I had created the bad energy; it had stemmed from me. Likewise, I could also deflect aggression by how I used my positive energy, and I was often able to defuse a volatile situation at the nightclub in this way. I could create and change situations through my thoughts and my own energy. This was all new and quite groundbreaking for me, but in a very positive way.

A permanent change in my place of work was needed, and thanks to the police this happened. Some undercover officers came into the nightclub one night and tried to order a meal. To have a late 2am liquor licence, you must serve food up until closing, and we were found in breach of the regulations and the owner was fined. I was deemed responsible because I was on duty, so I lost my job. It was divine timing; I was twenty-eight years of age when I left my nightclub manager career behind me.

I had received a very small golden handshake from the club owner as severance pay, and it paid for me to do a three-month intensive personal training and sports therapy course. I learnt all about the basics of nutrition, exercise, massage and therapy and injury rehabilitation. After successfully completing the course, I went to work for my friend as a personal trainer. At last I was honouring my body and mind a lot more, and it felt great.

I met a couple of friendly firemen at the gym; they always looked like they were having a lot of fun and both were super fit and healthy. I asked one of them what being a fireman was like, and he said it was great and that I should give it a go and join up myself. I could even look at being a personal trainer in the fire service if I didn't want to train as a firefighter. From that point on, I said to myself I was going to be a fireman.

I had suffered from asthma since I was a child, and everyone around me said this would prevent me from becoming a fireman. This left me feeling unsupported by my family and friends. Regardless, I persevered with my goal, and I knew I would succeed. It was very difficult to get into the fire services, and after eighteen months in 2002, I received a job offer to join the Surrey fire brigade in the Heathrow Airport area near London.

Before I joined the fire services, I had started to discover my latent mediumship abilities when I was undergoing the personal training. At the suggestion of a client I investigated meditation, and I started going to sessions at a Buddhist centre, where I would meditate for hours at a time. I also began attending group meditation lessons with a German woman. I loved this, and I had the most profound experiences when in a natural altered state of mind.

At the same time I was also making my rugby comeback, and unfortunately I was badly hurt. Nothing seemed to fix my injury, and it kept reoccurring, which prevented me from playing and training. A personal training client of mine knew of my recovery struggles and asked if I had ever had any healing work done. I misconstrued what healing was, and I had visions of some sort of faith healer.

My pain was constant, and I asked my client if she knew where I could seek some healing. Her husband turned out to be the healer in question, and I nervously went along to see him, having no concept of what he would do. Strangely, I knew deep down in myself that something special was going on here, but my mind really had no idea of what it was. I felt these emotions in another part of me, deep within my soul. I arrived, and the energy I felt in this man's presence and inside the room was almost tangible. I sat at the table feeling like a dog or a horse that shakes with anticipation or sheer excitement about something unknown that is about to happen to them.

I lay on the couch, and as he started to do his healing I began to see the most vivid colours possible, and I could feel this wonderful energy coming from him. He explained the energy, and it was so calming. Afterwards we spoke, and he said that my late grandfather was present. At that point I was both excited and petrified. Over the years I'd watched some TV shows about mediumship, and I had read some books that touched on the subject. Oddly, I wondered if I was a medium, because in all the books I had read I saw aspects of myself and I always thought, this is me.

The healer Stephen Smith told me I had within me the same abilities he had, and I should go to the Arthur Findlay College. You can see mediumship abilities in other people, and this is what he saw in me. Over the years I too have seen these same abilities in strangers, but I choose my words and timing very carefully about when or if I say anything to them. This man used to teach at the college with Glyn Edwards, who I hadn't heard of. Neither name nor place meant anything at all to me. I didn't even know there were Spiritualist churches; I'd never heard of them either.

In 2005 I reluctantly rang the college and requested a brochure about the courses on offer, which they mailed out to me. I noticed one called 'A Perfect Blending' being run by Janet Parker, and that is what I booked. I still knew absolutely nothing about what to do in order to be a medium. I had never sat in a development circle, I'd never attempted to do a reading of any kind and I had never set foot in a Spiritualist church. I was very nervous but also really excited about what was happening to me.

I was put into Janet's class, where she was teaching a group of mediums who were already working with their abilities. Even though I had no experience at all, this was the class that I was somehow placed in. I could do everything that was asked of me. I wasn't sure what I was doing, but the right answers were always forthcoming. The other students kept asking me if I was a total beginner, because everything just made sense and naturally seemed to work for me.

We had to do a psychic reading for someone in the class just from seeing their phone number. I wondered how that was even possible, and then Janet called me out to the front. I was so nervous, and she kindly held my hand. This relaxed me, and Janet said to say whatever I received in way of information. I was able to name the contents of a handbag that I 'saw', and everything was verified by the owner of the corresponding phone number. It was amazing!

As the week progressed we later started working with the spirit world, and I was to do mediumship for the first time. I told Janet I had never done anything like that before, and she was shocked that somehow I had been put into her advanced class. With Janet by my side, I followed her instructions and connected with a male spirit communicator. I was drawn to one woman in particular, and I knew she was the correct recipient. I shared the evidence given from her grandfather, as he relived his days flying during the war. Relevant names were given, and I was truly aware of the energy of the spirit world around me. I saw them as real, solid people, so I was in no doubt that this was all real. Janet's parting words to me were, 'We will get to know of you.'

After my wonderful experience at the college, I went home to visit my parents in Wales and said I had incredible news to tell them. I then announced, 'I'm a medium,' and they looked at me and said, 'Oh, that's nice.' I guess on a deeper level I was wanting to be welcomed back by my family as a real success. I had a deep-set need to gain their approval, and they supported me as best they could. Later on, my parents admitted they were petrified by what I had just told them. Each thought I had joined a religious cult, and neither knew what else to say.

The next year I talked my mum into attending the college with me, and she had the time of her life; she has since returned to do other courses there by herself. Later Mum joined a development circle in Aberystwyth, and she has really started to enjoy her own spiritual growth. My mother is an absolute natural-born medium, but she still tends to doubt her own abilities unless she is working with them at the college. Mum chooses not to practise as a medium, and I respect her for this; it's all about personal choice.

After my first few initial courses at Arthur Findlay College, I instinctively knew one day I would end up working there as a tutor. I didn't know at that stage how it was going to happen. I'm a believer that it's best to train with several different tutors, so that you can experience a more rounded approach to your mediumship, as each tutor is doing the same thing but in their own unique way, and I found it fascinating to see how they all worked. I was seeking a mentor, someone from the college I trusted completely. I had been doing more and more courses with Simon James, an English tutor who lives in Canada. I asked Simon if he would be my mentor, and he said that he normally didn't do that but to leave it with him. A year later on another course at the college, Simon took me aside and said he would work with me to reach a higher standard with my mediumship, and he also gently acknowledged that I wasn't ready to consider being a tutor myself. I understood this, but I knew that Simon could help to prepare me.

When I felt I was ready, I applied to attend an entry weekend for potential new tutors at Arthur Findlay, which I was accepted into. After that I completed another course called 'Willing to Work Week', and once you complete these requirements you are either invited, or not, to start the three-year teacher training at the college. It was both Simone Key and Simon James who invited me to join the teaching course in 2009, and I was so happy to accept my place. I have now been a qualified tutor at the college since 2012. Along the way I was fortunate enough to have other incredible teachers and mentors who have become great friends, including Eileen Davies and Tony Stockwell, among many others.

As a tutor, I do see some students who are desperate to become mediums but don't have the necessary abilities to do a spirit communication for a third party to understand. There are also those students who believe they are already mediums but in fact are not. It's always a very difficult situation for the tutor when this happens, and I remember when I first started my own mediumship development we were told in quite a brutal way by some tutors that you either had mediumship abilities or you didn't. I don't work in that way with my own students. I believe that whoever is taking a course is there for personal reasons, and sometimes they need to have this unique experience for themselves. I will always talk with my students to guide them further in any way I can, and sometimes they realise themselves that mediumship is not for them. I feel it is essential to always speak to them in a very positive light.

My father has gone from being not really interested in my mediumship to now showing a keen interest. When I started teaching I was doing quite a lot of work with Tony Stockwell, who is quite famous with many people in Aberystwyth, who worship him quite a bit. As soon as Dad knew of Tony's popularity, he would say to these locals, 'My boy does that work too, and he's one of the best!' I once returned home to visit, and Dad had taken it on himself to book me in for a private sitting to a local woman. I was shocked.

I once went back to Aberystwyth for a week of mediumship teaching workshops, and I gave private sittings in the evenings. One night I performed a demonstration at the local hall. My whole family came along, including my brother, and loads of local people. My paternal grandfather was one of the spirit communicators that night, and Dad finally understood the power of mediumship and how being reconnected with a loved one affects you emotionally. This was the first time he had ever seen me work as a medium.

When I first started my mediumship development I lived a double life at work, where absolutely no-one knew what I did after hours, which was making me feel quite stressed and sick. Initially after my mid-week shift finished and I had a church demonstration to do, I would get dressed into my suit in the car, because I didn't want to have to explain what I was doing. On a Sunday morning after finishing a Saturday-night shift, I thought it was safe to change into my suit at the fire station. When asked why I was putting a suit on, I would say I was going to a christening – I must have gone to dozens of christenings each year!

I made a conscious decision to not broadcast what I was doing, but not to lie about it either. I was floored when my boss asked one day, 'So, how long have you been a medium?' He had seen something on my Facebook page, and I was shocked, but we had a chat about things, and even though he was very old-school, once I knew he was on side with me I knew it would be okay with everyone else at the station. I had been a fireman for about five years when my colleagues found out about my mediumship and my double life.

Nowadays I tell everyone at work what I do and where I'm going when I head off to teach at the college on my weeks off, and everyone is fine with it. I once had a situation with one guy at work who was very hard-nosed about everything in life. I was cooking my lunch in the mess area, and he stormed in and said, 'Do you talk to dead people?' and I said yes. He said 'F*%k off' and stormed out, and then he kept coming in and out, again and again. His behaviour was quite manic, and he said, 'You're trying to tell me ...' I asked to him to stop, as I wasn't trying to tell him anything. I told him he was asking me questions and I was trying to answer them but that he kept storming off, so I asked him what he wanted to know. At that moment another colleague walked in, and my hard-nosed mate asked him if he knew what I did. He answered, 'What mediumship?' and this diffused everything completely, and we are friends now.

My mother remembers that when I was between five and ten I would sit alone having conversations with unseen people. She thought I was just being weird, but now that she understands mediumship she knows what I was doing. I wish I could remember who I was talking to, but I can't. I think I lost that knowledge when I intentionally shut everything down as a young teenager. It's such a shame when this happens, and I know that it is so common for many youngsters who are mediums in the making.

It's becoming harder for me now to book my teaching weeks in advance at the college because the fire service is becoming smaller and smaller, and I'm needed at work more often. I'm also currently in my third year of five training to be a body psychotherapist, so life is very busy. With body psychotherapy, we look at deep trauma within the patient where emotions get trapped inside the body, as well as in the mind. Everything that has happened to us in our lives stays with us, and the body holds on to this trauma and subsequent emotions. Many of these problems stem from the formative years, and through a process of normal talking therapy and movement, biodynamic massage and vegetative therapy, we can start to encourage the living essence of the patients to express themselves and become fully alive again.

Many illnesses manifest because past traumas are not dealt with, and much of this understandably ties in with mediumship as well. I can now look at the embodiment of energy in the individual, and I can see that many mediums are not fully grounded or fully present in this world; they are trying constantly to escape to the spirit world and to spend time in realms of fantasy, and none of this is healthy for them. Mediums are living human beings, and we all need to live in the human world and its constraints. This course has given me the tools and awareness to help other mediums to become well again, if they find themselves escaping the 'now' of everyday life.

My busy life does not allow me to perform as many demonstrations as I did when I first started out. I prefer now to not accept any offers to do demonstrating in the Spiritual churches, because I don't want to let people down. My work as a fireman can obviously be very unpredictable, regarding when my shifts will finish, and I'm always prone to running late or not making it to any of my commitments at all.

Over the years, I have been fortunate enough to demonstrate in Australia, The Netherlands, Italy, Switzerland, Denmark and in many locations in the United Kingdom. I have never created my own work abroad; I have always been invited by other mediums who I know and trust, and we travel and teach together. It's been an amazing experience, and I hope to do more travel and teaching in future years. I prefer not to do lots of private sittings, and I feel that many mediums do too many readings in a single day; we were never meant to do such a high turnover. The great mediums in the past would only ever do one or two readings a day, and some would only do a few per week.

We do an unnatural number of readings at the college as part of what's required as a tutor. During a week-long course we do private sittings and mediumship assessments for the students, platform demonstrations and more daily readings in a classroom situation. It's not natural to connect so often with the spirit world, and I feel that you shouldn't work in that way all the time.

When I was younger I was afraid to die, but because of my mediumship I no longer feel that way. At one time I felt the need for a 'dignified death', almost as if I had to die saving someone else, but now I think this might have been a bit of an ego thing really. My whole concept has changed now, and I know there is something huge waiting for me. I'm excited to explore it. Having said that, I'm also very keen to continue living, as I still have so many things to do here on Earth.

Life is great. I'm engaged to Kristin, who I met at the college when she was studying as a student. We are renovating our home in Shoreham, near Brighton on the coast, and I continue to teach part-time at the college and work full-time in the fire services.

Professional firefighter, medium, healer, tutor, body psychotherapist (in training)
Age, 49
Shoreham, United Kingdom

Instagram/Facebook @andrewmanship

Chapter twelve

Adam Berry

Adam and I met in July 2019 at the college, and I was immediately struck by his kind, gentle and shy nature. It was after seeing Adam do an outstanding communication at a student platform demonstration that I wanted to know more about him. Adam's reading was absolutely amazing; his connection to the spirit communicator was so strong, and the evidence he shared with the recipient was incredible. Adam's level of experience was obvious, though he was still a student at the college at the time. Challenges are aplenty in Adam's life, and I was struck by what he shared with me, such a personal and open story that may surprise many. Adam is from the United Kingdom, and he works full-time in construction management and is now a newly graduated tutor at the college.

As a child I could only be described as being very sensitive, shy and introverted. I was never an aggressive little boy; I was quite the opposite, and I really needed to be encouraged to become involved in things. I somehow always held back. On reflection I realise that I was also very intuitive from an early age, but actually seeing what I now know is the spirit world, well, that didn't happen for me.

I must have been five or six years old, and I was in reception level of my school at Tottington South County Primary School in the United Kingdom. It's strange what you remember as a child, but I can clearly recall a picture of a 'birthday train' with twelve carriages on the wall, each carriage being labelled January through to December. Each of the student's names was written on the carriage that showed the month of their birth. I could always remember every single month of birth for every child in my class, and I never understood why.

My birthday was in January, and I was the only child in my class with a birthday that month. Years on, every time I met someone new I would think about this birthday train and its carriages and whether this newcomer reminded me of someone in my class. If they did, I was able to predict accurately what their month of birth was.

My family life was very different to most, and I feel that this also had an impact on how I saw myself and how I fitted in. Life was never really that straightforward for me. My parents, Pete and Laura, married and had me when they were young, and when I was two years old I went to live permanently with my mother's parents. My grandparents were known to me as 'Mum' and 'Dad'. They became my legal guardians, and my mother's siblings, my aunt and uncle, were called my 'brother' and 'sister'. I loved them all very much, and I was happy to refer to them this way.

My unusual upbringing prompted some inherent feelings of rejection, but my parents gave me much love and a safe and secure home to grow up in. I adored my sister, Sarah, who was thirteen years older than me. My brother, Jamie, was eight years older. When I was growing up, Sarah always had a real interest in things that were quite magical to me: she had things like Tarot cards, crystals, pendulums and horoscopes, none of which I understood. Nevertheless, I was very intrigued by them. I loved being in Sarah's company, and she was always very influential in my life. At school Sarah taught me my times tables. She helped me a lot with my homework and always encouraged me with all aspects of my education.

Sarah used to let me touch her Tarot cards, and I would sneak into her room to play with them. I remember taking the cards into the dining room when a family friend was over. This visitor was making fun of me by saying, 'Come on, Adam, tell me what my future is.' I turned over the Lovers card and I said, 'There's two lovers here and one in the background.' I didn't understand the meaning of the card, and I was taking the picture quite literally. Everyone was laughing at me, so once again I withdrew and kept to myself. It turned out later that this woman was having an affair, and in hindsight this was a very profound experience.

As a child I always had great intuition for healing people and animals. I somehow had an innate 'knowing' of how to heal both. I could make the family Yorkshire terrier go from growling to a state of calm, then I could make him go to sleep. I could do this by just by placing my hands above the dog, and I believed I had a power that ran through me that could heal others.

Growing up I still had contact with my birth father, who lived on a farm not far from where I lived with my parents in Bury, Lancashire. Thursday night was our night to get together, and as I got older we would head to the pub on Sunday at lunchtime to play pool, and this became our norm. My biological father had severe paranoid schizophrenia, and his life was a difficult one. His own mother had died when he was young, and this greatly affected his mental health and wellbeing, and he missed her terribly.

On the last Thursday night that we were together, I sensed that something wasn't right with him; he seemed to be going through the all too familiar pattern of psychosis. When I visited my father the following Sunday he said, 'I'll miss you when you're gone,' and I said, 'Don't be silly, you idiot; I'll see you next Thursday.' The next day he was hospitalised once again in the same psychiatric hospital I had visited him in many, many times throughout my life. I realise now I had a lot of issues to deal with due to my father's mental illness, as it deprived me in so many ways of having a happier childhood. Because of this upset and frustration about yet another visit to the psychiatric hospital, I didn't go and see him. My parents got a phone call from the police to say that my dad was missing from the hospital; I already knew instinctively that he was dead.

We found out afterwards that my father's body had been found by two children who saw him in the river. He had suffered a heart attack while trying to cross, and had subsequently drowned. Apparently, someone had accidently left the main door of the ward unlocked, and he left the hospital and escaped. Dad was only forty-two years old when he died, and I was seventeen. His loss was like a train crash for me, the impact was so great, but it did make me really want to believe in another life after this one. Without any understanding of why I did this, I wrote my father a letter and shared my deepest feelings and said my last goodbye. I then burnt the letter, knowing that my message would somehow reach my dad. It all felt so instinctively right to do this.

I was so angry with the hospital for not keeping my father locked away safely, and I struggled to deal with his loss and the circumstances of how he passed. He had died because of the nursing staff's sheer carelessness in not properly checking that the door to the ward was locked. He was meant to be safe in there, and he wasn't.

Since I had my first alcoholic drink as a thirteen-year-old I had always been a greedy drinker. My friends would share a bottle of cider, and I always needed to have my own, and I drank it all by myself. After Dad passed my drinking became out of control, and I developed a chronic problem with alcohol. I was completely off the rails in my behaviour. My grief was immense and all-consuming, and a year later I ended up being sent to the same psychiatric hospital that my dad was placed in, to go through an alcohol rehabilitation and detox program. I was also treated for anxiety and depression. I was diagnosed incorrectly as having bipolar, and they started treating me with lithium.

What angered me more was that I was being kept in exactly the same ward with the same nursing staff who had failed to keep my dad safe. It was here that I was pumped full of antipsychotic drugs, and no-one considered for a moment that I was just a bereft young man grieving the loss of his dead father and not some psychotic youth. I was eighteen years old when I was discharged from the hospital, and I now had to work at staying off alcohol and at getting my life back together. I joined Alcoholics Anonymous (AA), who had meetings every Saturday night at the hospital. My visits there were on and off over a three-month period.

AA really helped me to know who I was, and much of what they taught me was very beneficial. I attended all of the meetings as required, but I was always too scared to stand up and speak at any of sessions. There was a man there called 'Big Mike', who was my sponsor. He was thirty-five years sober and was in his eighties. Even though we were decades apart in age, our lives were so similar: he was raised by his grandparents too, and we had both experienced many of the same life patterns. Mike helped me in so many ways, and I've always been very grateful to him and others, who I still have contact with today.

I met my best friend, Clare, when I was sixteen on a rare night out with my brother and his friends. Clare read Tarot cards and understood star signs. She was twenty-three years old, and we have become lifelong friends ever since. Clare and I talked all night, and even though we had only just met there was a real connection between us. It was Clare who first introduced me to the Spiritualist Church. Clare had been hearing strange voices in her head and decided to seek answers by visiting a Spiritualist church. Soon after, she started attending a spiritual awareness circle that was held by the church.

While Clare was attending the circle group some other friends and I would wait at her place, and the moment she arrived home everyone was wanting to know what happened at circle. I was fascinated by everything that Clare shared with us. When I was nineteen I went with Clare and eight of her friends to the Spiritualist church to see a mediumship demonstration. This was my first time in a Spiritualist church, and I was intrigued. I thought that the medium must talk to the same people each week, because how else could she know so much about them and their loved ones? I have always had a sceptical side to me; this took over completely, and I was thinking logically.

Over a cup of tea and a biscuit afterwards, we all grilled the poor medium and asked loads of questions. We were totally unaware that the proper Church protocol is not to interrogate the medium, and it is very much frowned upon. Clare was asking the medium so many questions, and in the end the woman decided to go around to each of us and give some information. When it was my turn, the medium gave my dad's name and told me something personal about him. I was both shocked and amazed, so I kept going back to the church to get whatever information I could relating to my father in spirit.

I started to also attend the spiritual awareness classes that Clare went to, but I could never see anything when we meditated, and this worried me. Other students saw unicorns, rainbows and waterfalls, and I got nothing like this from the meditations. I kept attending the classes for eighteen months, and I saw the other students progressing and starting to connect with the spirit world. I was always too quiet to put myself forward at the classes, but something kept me there.

Our original teacher left the circle, and a new one took over. This new teacher turned out to be a real bully, but only towards me. I still didn't know the difference between a psychic reading and a mediumship reading, and the teacher didn't seem to know the difference either. I never went back to that circle again because of the horrible treatment I received. Slowly all of the other students left as well, and it was eventually disbanded.

When I was in my twenties I started reading Tarot cards and doing one-on-one psychic readings for people. This was fine, and I thought this was all I would do with my abilities. I began doing free Tarot card readings for the girls in the office and for other staff members at the construction company where I worked. I enjoyed reading Tarot cards, and when I was in my late twenties I did some low-paid readings and began some reiki study.

As things progressed I got involved in healing through attending a Christian Spiritualist church. Then I started attending the Spiritualist National Union church as well. The only issue with 'church' for me was not the spirit world, but the worshipping of God. I had always had problems with my perception of who we were actually worshipping, and as a child my understanding of God was him sitting on a throne throwing thunderbolts at people who did the wrong thing. I had always believed there was something more to this life; I just didn't know what it was.

After attending the Christian Spiritualist church in Bury, I was encouraged by friends to get up on the platform to do a reading during the church service. I felt I was ready to do my first public demonstration, as I had been continuing with my mediumship development over the years in different development circles. I started the communication with a female spirit contact. She presented herself as being beautifully dressed and pristine looking, then she showed me images of herself putting on make-up. There was a glass of wine sitting beside her.

I was drawn to a woman sitting in the congregation, and I instinctively knew this woman in spirit was her mother. Suddenly I 'saw' the spirit woman looking bedraggled; her lipstick was smeared and she appeared like she had been dragged through a hedge backwards. I shared this, and everyone started laughing, but the recipient in the audience wouldn't accept any of the information I gave. She said no to everything that I received and gave as evidence. I was crushed by her responses, and I found it hard to accept that all I had been given from spirit was wrong.

I was mortified by this experience, and for two long weeks I was left wondering if I was actually a medium. A fortnight later the same recipient came to me at the church and said she could take every piece of evidence I gave to her in the reading, but she was too embarrassed to acknowledge publicly that her mother was an alcoholic. This did help me slightly, but it took me another six years to get back up on the platform because my confidence as a medium was completely gone. I was in my early thirties when I finally started doing platform work again.

I still attended workshops and continued going to church services, but I gave no readings. A huge turning point came after I met a medium called Kenneth Hartley, who was a real Spiritualist guru at the time. Initially, I thought that Kenneth was an odd old man who spoke in a trance state with a Texan accent. I'd heard that Kenneth had what's called the 'Jesus effect' on people, because all who meet him feel that their lives are changed just by being in his presence; and this happened for me. I was in a difficult personal relationship, and I decided to end it. Something just came over me that made me realise that I had to make significant changes and take control of my life.

I was depressed and always anxious for the future but still caught up in the past. I could never fully enjoy the moment because I was always waiting to have someone take it away from me and for the badness to come again. Meeting Kenneth was like a wave of positivity coming over me, and I started to feel stronger and more self-assured in all that I did and said. At work I asked for, and received, a pay rise, and my family and friends saw a real change in me.

In 2005 my friend Robin suggested that we both do a week-long course at the Arthur Findlay College. While we were waiting for the plane in Blackpool we ran into a tutor called Jill Harland, who Robin knew from previous visits to the college. We decided to all have coffee together, and Jill asked permission to do a reading for Robin, because she was aware of the presence of Robin's mother in spirit, who had very recently passed. I have never experienced anything so moving and wonderful as this reading. Jill took mediumship to a level I had never seen before, and the emotion of the connection was felt by me too, even though the reading wasn't mine.

Robin had somehow arranged for me to train in Glyn Edwards' class, a well renowned and highly respected English medium, who is now in spirit. It was Glyn who helped me to believe that there was more to me and my mediumship abilities. One evening in class Glyn said to the packed room, 'If only young Adam knew how much potential he has.' I was mortified and so embarrassed to be singled out in front of everyone.

During a group session I made a connection with a male in spirit. I was amazed by the clarity of what I saw, and the girl who I was reading for was in tears. It was her deceased boyfriend who had never come through in a reading before. I could physically perform all of his actions; I knew his name, and I could describe the interior of where he lived. I was shocked that she understood everything, and it was then that I truly appreciated that I could do mediumship.

In 2011, I married my husband, Shaun, who is very supportive of me and my mediumship but is not a medium himself. Shaun has been my rock, and I've been so very lucky to share my life with him. I couldn't do all that I do with my mediumship work without Shaun's constant support, and for this I am very grateful. Shaun's father gave him some money, and Shaun insisted that I use the money to return to Arthur Findlay College because he always noticed how my eyes lit up when I talked about the place. I returned to the college, this time to do a course called 'Embracing the Spirit' with Tony Stockwell, another wonderful English medium, and it was another life-changing experience.

I was still a quiet student, but many tutors saw my potential. It was recommended to me that I contact a highly regarded medium called Mavis Pittilla, who happened to live nearby to me. An opportunity arose for me to attend a mediumship course that was being given by Mavis in the town of Disley. I can remember Mavis hovering her hand over my back saying, 'He has a good power'. To be honest I didn't really know what this meant, but it sounded very positive. During that weekend course my class tutor was Janet Parker, who I also found to be very inspirational and also a wonderful teacher. Mavis did a private reading for me, and she said that in three years I would be a professional platform medium. This all seemed impossible at the time, but Mavis's reading turned out to be totally accurate.

I was intrigued that Janet Parker was also an ordained minister in the SNU. I checked her website and noticed she performed spiritual naming ceremonies, so I contacted her about having one. Janet and her husband, Trevor, drove to the Aquarius Christian Spiritualist Church that I had attended for many years in Bury, and my wonderful naming ceremony took place with Janet officiating.

For me this was such a special event. I had invited all of my family and close friends along and, as requested, they all brought a flower along with them as part of the ritual of this spiritual service. Janet gave me the name of 'Peter', which means 'the rock', as I had been a rock to many people. My own father in spirit was also called Peter, and to me this was so profound. There is much personal meaning in my new spiritual name, and that day I truly accepted that I am a Spiritualist.

I had a life-changing dream, and Mavis Pittilla was in it. We were both on a train platform together, and Mavis said, 'Are you coming on my course, young man?' I was feeling stressed in the dream because

Mavis looked disappointed that I hadn't responded about attending her course. I knew that I had work commitments at that time, and I woke up feeling extremely anxious about the dream and this unknown course that I was supposed to be going to. It was only 5.30am, and I lay there wondering how I could get out of work. At that point, I still didn't know what the course was about. I got out of bed and looked up Mavis's website and found that the course was 'Mediumship Mentorship'. It was like a thunderbolt going through me, and I knew that I needed to apply, as the course outline covered everything I had always wanted to learn, even after all these years of mediumship study.

I was interviewed and approved by Mavis, and the course was the best thing I have ever studied. It brought everything together for me, and Mavis and her partner, Jean, nurtured me and my sensitivity. During this time working with Mavis, I took my first solo divine service and demonstration of mediumship at the Rawtenstall Spiritualist Church, and little did I know that one day I would be the president of this church.

Mavis had invited me to teach with her at the Manchester Spiritualist Church, and on arrival she gave me a pad and pen and asked me to psychically assess all the students before the course started. I was to 'look' into the energy of each person and write down what I saw relating to the student's spiritual development. The students arrived for the class, and I could only describe them by their clothing, as I didn't know anyone's names. After an initial welcome, Mavis went around the room and verbally asked each student where they felt they were at with their own development. As each student responded, their answers were exactly what I had already observed and written down. I was shocked by the results, but Mavis was delighted and said, 'I am proving to you that you are a teacher.' I'm extremely grateful to her for all of her wonderful encouragement.

My sister, Sarah, always wanted to own a crystal shop, and the plan was that I would do the Tarot card and mediumship readings and she would sell the crystals, books and cards. We loved to talk about these plans, but tragically in 2013 Sarah died of heart failure due to medication complications; she was only forty-five years of age. Her death was like the second train crash in my life. We were very close, and she had always supported me in coping with my father's passing. I stopped my mediumship for a while after she died; I couldn't continue because of my immense grief.

Roy Foreman, a local medium and friend, helped me get my mediumship going again and even organised an evening at the Rawtenstall Spiritualist Church, where he stood next to me on the platform for added support. Roy had invited all of the people in attendance. It was to help me feel confident again as a medium at what he called a 'sympathetic congregation'. This act of kindness that Roy gifted me was one I will never forget, as it helped me so much to come back into the service of spirit.

In 2016 I was recommended by a friend to apply for the Gordon Higginson Memorial Scholarship at the Barbanell Centre in Stafford. I was initially short-listed and was overwhelmed when I won it. This wonderful award granted me six weekly courses at the Arthur Findlay College over a three-year period, including the teacher training course and other academic courses. I've completed my scholarship and have gained my Certificate of Recognition with the SNU, as a speaker, demonstrator and teacher (at Church level). In early 2021, I completed my tutor training at the college, enabling me to teach the students, and I am immensely proud of this achievement.

My life has changed so much, but in a very positive way both personally and in my mediumship. Spiritualism has helped me understand the power that is greater than all of us. I realised my mediumship had changed after my sister, Sarah, died. Her passing gave me a greater understanding that it is the spirit world that decides what it wants and needs to communicate in a reading and not what the recipient or medium wants to hear. With mediumship, emotions need to be touched and memories shared, thereby allowing a celebration and healing between the two worlds to take place. As mediums we are here to give spirit a voice and the opportunity to help them prove that they are very much alive and there is no real death.

Looking back, the Department of Social Security had basically written me off as a young man. They assessed me as being someone who would never work in regular paid employment, and I would be on government benefits indefinitely, due to my complex issues with alcoholism. I proved them wrong. I did volunteer work at nineteen and then started work in the construction industry at twenty-one, where I'm now a site supervisor working more on the technical side, which I really enjoy.

My life is now full, rich and very rewarding, and I am very thankful to all of the many people who have helped me along the way.

Medium, tutor and works full-time in construction management
Age, 40
Lancashire, North West England

www.adamberrymedium.com
adam.berry1981@gmail.com

Chapter thirteen

LYNN PARKER

Lynn was one of my tutors at the college in 2016, and I attended some of her wonderful tutorials in 2019. Lynn is a fabulous tutor and compassionate medium. I had a very memorable one-on-one reading with Lynn in 2016; it was during that sitting when Lynn communicated with my son, Sam. Sam shared lots of wonderful evidence and memories with Lynn, and one piece of evidence was particularly pertinent. Lynn said that Sam was talking about a woman called Toni, who was very instrumental in my mediumship and influential in my life since Sam's passing. That 'Toni' is none other than Toni Reilly, who was the reason I attended the college in the first place! Lynn lives in the United Kingdom and is a full-time medium and tutor at the college.

I come from a pretty normal background. My parents were working-class people, and we lived in the village of Congleton, Cheshire, in the United Kingdom. My mother, Millicent, was a cleaner at the local school, and she also worked as a sewing machinist in a local factory in Congleton. John, my father, was a sewing machine engineer, and he worked in the same factory as Mum. I've only ever lived in two houses in my entire life, the family home with Mum, Dad and my younger sister, Jill, and my current home in Crewe, after marrying my husband, Andrew, in 1983.

Sadly, our mother died from cancer when I was only nineteen and Jill was just sixteen. Since that time I haven't ever felt Mum around me in spirit. I had a sitting many years ago, and the medium said that Mum was there, but to be honest the information she gave didn't prove to me that it was my mother, so I didn't accept that it was her. In 2013 my lovely dad passed away from heart failure. He was eighty-three when he died.

I have always been aware of the spirit world since I was a child. I would see people disappearing through the walls and walking across the bedroom, and this was all a bit scary, as I was alone in the room with them. When I was in my late twenties, I went along with some friends who were having a mediumship reading done, and when we were there, I was told by the medium that I had a natural ability to develop as a medium myself, but she never told me what I should do about it. This knowledge didn't really explain the strange experiences I'd been having, and it actually created more questions and confusion about how I should deal with what the medium had said.

Our family were Church of England, and my godmother, Betsy, introduced me to Spiritualism. She went regularly to the Spiritualist church services. For me, it felt like going home when I went through the Spiritualist church doors for the first time. I was in my early thirties, and although I had attended other churches over the years, I had previously never felt any real connection with what they spoke about. This all changed with the Spiritualist Church; it felt welcoming and relaxed, and here people hugged one another. This surprised me, as it certainly didn't happen at the Church of England services.

What I experienced really touched something within my soul, almost as if this is what I had been waiting for all my life. I started going to the Crewe Spiritualist Church, because I had questions about my potential for mediumship. I discovered the church ran a circle, and I had no idea what this involved or how it worked. The circle was run by a medium called Stan, who was also the church president and whose family were all mediums too. It was here that I learnt how to develop my natural mediumship abilities, just as the medium had suggested years earlier in my reading.

I was fascinated in watching the mediums work on the platform during the church services. My mediumship tuition seems so different to that of many other mediums, as I didn't attend any courses or workshops outside of the mediumship development classes run by the Spiritualist church. I had no idea what the word 'psychic' even meant, as the church circle only worked with the spirit world. One day I saw a list go up on the noticeboard at the church asking for people who were interested in taking part in a new mediumship development group. I asked Stan, who would be teaching the group, and he replied, 'You'!

It was like my destiny was being helped along by outside influences. I took on the running of the new circle, and I enjoyed teaching the students attending. A friend phoned one day and said, 'I've put your name down to take a service at the Northwich church.'

It was never my plan to take the church services. It wasn't what I wanted, but I took the service regardless, and everything just unfolded after that. I was very much following an unknown path, but it all felt very right. By this stage I was in my thirties and now a working platform medium.

I don't think I ever realised what the journey of mediumship would entail. For someone who liked routine and security, the twists and turns of finding out about my mediumship meant I had to find out a whole lot about myself. I realised I needed to adapt more readily to change and become extra flexible as a person, while pacing myself better in managing my workload. Mediums seem to have a problem with saying no, and through personal experience, I have learnt to say no more often and to take more time to consider things fully. Through my mediumship I have found an inner strength, and I sometimes find it easier to do things on my own rather than to ask for other people's opinions.

Growing up I went to university at Chester College, in Cheshire, and I trained as a primary school teacher. When I finished my bachelor of education, I worked in a private kindergarten in my hometown of Congleton. My work was put on hold while I had our four children, two girls and identical twin boys. When my twin boys were small, I started to work at a preschool, and then a friend told me about another job doing administration work in the office of a dating agency. I managed to understand a lot about people in that job, and I also learnt not to judge anyone by their physical appearance.

During this time I was already juggling my mediumship readings and my church work. I was a committee member and also running the awareness groups and an open circle. I was out most evenings running church services at many of the different churches in the North West of England. I was travelling quite long distances to do private readings in other people's homes and in our own home too. With the bigger groups I found it was easier to go to them. I also worked at charity nights in pubs doing one-on-one readings and mediumship demonstrations. I don't work like this any longer, but they were all good experiences for me.

Some of the charity events I did with other mediums, as audience numbers were larger. As a group we would advertise the events, and everyone attending paid an admission for the platform demonstrations and separately for the one-on-one private sittings.

Some evenings I wouldn't get home until after midnight, and then I would have to go to work the following morning at the dating agency. It was very hard work, but it gave me a good grounding in my mediumship. I was in my early forties when I made the decision to become a full-time medium.

I started to attend the occasional mediumship workshop outside of my church, and I went to a centre in South Wales with my friend, Marie, and at this workshop she told me about the Arthur Findlay College. I think Marie had found out about the college from the internet because she hadn't actually been there herself, but she told me it sounded like an amazing place and how I should go to the college. Marie had begun to develop her own mediumship, but she didn't do much more with it. We lost touch over the years, and I sometimes wonder if I was meant to meet Marie in order to find out about the college. I was about forty-five years old when I finally went there.

The first course I took at the college was a weekend about teaching mediumship. I then went for a couple of weeks each year, and one of my first courses was with Simon James, who was my tutor, and another week I was with Simone Key. Both are wonderful mediums and teachers. I was definitely not a confident student; I was always the last person to volunteer, and I always doubted my abilities. Though by this stage I'd been teaching my own students, doing private sittings, public demonstrations and taking church services for many years. The formal training at the college helped me to sharpen my skills and filled in many of the gaps I had in my existing knowledge.

Never for a moment had I considered teaching at the college. I initially attended the weekend course about teaching mediumship so I could gauge if I was teaching in the right way at my circle groups. I later discovered that the particular weekend of my course was the 'access weekend' for the tutor training scheme at the college. It was suggested that I put my name down on the very long waiting list, so I decided to do so. That was in the November, and amazingly in the following March I began the 'Tutor Training' program at Arthur Findlay College. I never set out to become a medium or a tutor, but looking back new opportunities just arose when I needed them to. Learning to go with them was the more challenging part!

In the early days I didn't charge for any readings, and I had quite a big battle within myself about getting paid or not. I was apprehensive about asking for money, because this was an ability that had been given to me to help people and not something to make money out of. I still feel like that now to a certain extent. I began by charging a small amount of money and people paid it, and I continued to get more and more bookings. Finally, after a lot of soul searching, I came to the realisation that if didn't charge I would have to find other work to make ends meet, and I would have less time to serve the spirit world.

As a person I'm quite a home bird, and I have never been worried or bored about being at home. My life now means I'm away from home a lot during the year. I'm fortunate that I work about twelve to fifteen weeks a year at the college. I also work teaching and demonstrating in Germany, The Netherlands, Switzerland and Finland. I always swore that I wouldn't become one of those mediums who was home for three days, then away again; how wrong I was!

At the workshops I run in Europe, I work with groups of students where I teach evidential mediumship, trance and animal communication. I usually do a mediumship demonstration while I'm there, and I also do private sittings, so it's pretty intensive. One of the places where I teach is in Hamburg, Germany, and here we hold the seminars at an operating funeral parlour. It's rather different to most venues, as we have to walk past the coffins on sale each time we have a coffee and meal break. Having said this, it's actually a lovely place to work, and the energy there is very healing.

With my classes in Europe the students are taught in English, and I use translators to share what I'm teaching them; it slows down the process, but it works well. When things are tough or I'm feeling insecure about not having enough work, I sometimes wish that I had a regular job, but I wouldn't ever give up my mediumship. I'm fortunate in that my work is quite regular, but there is always the underlying feeling of what I would do if it stopped. During 2020 and 2021, my work has had to change to teaching online and doing private sittings, courses and demonstrating via Zoom because of Covid-19.

I'm fortunate I haven't lost any family or friends because of my mediumship, but I would say that a couple of my friends' attitudes towards me have changed. Sometimes there seems to be an awkwardness if I mention my work. Not in a negative way, but maybe due to a lack of understanding about what mediumship is. With some friends it's not a topic of conversation, but others ask me where I am going to next on my travels. Most of the friends I have now are interested in spirituality and mediumship, and it's always a pleasure to discuss mediumship with them. It is my passion, so I love to talk with others about it, but I am also very respectful when I'm with people who are not interested.

My husband, Andrew, is supportive about what I do, though he doesn't attend church at all. He has been invaluable over the years, minding the children and pets, which has made it easier for me to do my mediumship work. Three of our grown children are engineers, so they are very logically minded and are not really interested in what I do; they are supportive, just not involved. Andrew and the children have all seen me demonstrate on the platform at various times. They don't ask any questions about my work and probably think it's a strange job.

I believe some people have a stereotypical idea about mediums: the idea that we sit in the dark and conjure up the dead. I think it also depends on the enquirer's own background, religion and belief system. There is a misconception that evil spirits can come and possess mediums. Even though we know this cannot be the case, it is important to take these fears seriously when voiced by people. As soon as you explain that mediumship is about love, energy and life after death, their minds generally begin to open up to new possibilities.

We can never force our own understanding of mediumship onto others. This is something that some people find difficult to understand, because maybe they are expecting to be lectured and potentially converted. Lack of education about mediumship has also led people over the years to believe that mediums are mind readers, and therefore no thoughts are private. I think many of the bad attitudes and misunderstandings come from people who lack any knowledge about what mediumship really is. Life is about perception, and if we offer a different aspect for them to think about, this can change their outlook and understanding in a positive way.

I think there is confusion between the words 'medium' and 'psychic'. Some people think that mediums predict the lottery numbers or when they will be moving house. Again, education is very necessary in order to explain and promote what we actually do as mediums, with emphasis on the fact that everything about mediumship includes healing and love. The realisation that we encourage people to make up their own minds as to whether they believe we can communicate with the dead or not can change people's perceptions.

I am a Spiritualist; that is my religion. In the Spiritualist religion we have churches that are run by volunteers, and the religion as a whole is also largely run by volunteers, apart from the president of the Spiritualist National Union and the administration staff at the head office. My training is ongoing, and I'm now an officiant of the SNU, which means I'm qualified to officiate at naming ceremonies, weddings and funerals. These services can be conducted in Spiritualist churches and other venues.

I am currently training to become a minister of the SNU, and I see my work as a Spiritualist and medium as a lifelong commitment. Pastoral care is a vital part of being a member of the SNU ministry, as well as chaplaincy work in hospitals, hospices, universities and prisons. All future ministers are invited to train to become ministers of the church; it is not something one can apply to become. Becoming a minister was not something I had ever considered previously, but the more I embraced the philosophy and religion of Spiritualism, the more I felt drawn to it. It wasn't a conscious choice; it was more connected to the evolution and unfoldment coming from within.

Apart from a couple of home circles I went to in my early training, much of what I learnt about mediumship was from watching other mediums work at the church services. The home circles were very informal and were really a case of sitting in silence and seeing what we got, which really wasn't a lot; back then I had no clue how to blend with the spirit world. Although I enjoyed these circle groups, I think it was the more structured teaching at the college that helped me to unfold my mediumship in the best possible way. I think that natural ability needs to be nurtured, but at some point we need to learn how to develop those already existing abilities.

At first I had a real hesitation (and I still do occasionally) about the question, 'What do you do for a living?' I'm never ashamed of saying that I'm a medium, but because my mediumship is so precious to me, I want people to properly understand what it means. Occasionally, I might say that I teach adults, and if they ask what I teach, then I say mediumship. Intuitively, you know when to fully disclose what you do. For me, there is an insecurity where I worry that people might see me differently or judge me in some way because of my mediumship work. I am now more confident, of course, but I think that in the early years other people's perceptions mattered a lot to me.

I love all aspects of mediumship. I'm very flexible with the different modalities, and I wouldn't say that I have any one specialism. I am always inspired by the spirit world, and I learn so much every time I work, even after twenty-five years! I also work with animal communication and shamanism, which I love. Animal communication includes working with living animals, or by just knowing the animal's name, or by seeing a photograph of them. Working this way, animals can express their opinions, which can help to improve the relationship between the animal and owner. It can also help resolve any issues an animal might have from its past; for example, if it is a rescue animal.

Animals in the spirit world communicate to show us they live on as well, just as humans do. We can also work with animal spirit guides, which are part of our team of helpers in the spirit world. Shamanism is about spirit in all things; it's about our connection to nature, to the Earth and to our ancestors and what we can learn from them. It includes healing, journeying (which is similar to meditation), ceremony, storytelling and trying to find a part of this as our authentic self.

I also love the art and creative weeks I work on at the college, but I have to say that I'm not a spirit artist myself. On creative weeks we use a variety of materials to encourage students to develop their sensitivity and to help in allowing the spirit within to unfold. Working with creativity also allows the spirit world the opportunity to influence the students while using materials such as paint, wax, pastels, clay, items from nature, as well as the written and spoken word. I think in a way these courses take me back to my roots of kindergarten teaching, with the creativity aspect.

I also teach on trance weeks, which are always very interesting, but I prefer to use the term 'altered state'. Every time we work with our sensitivity, we are in an altered state of consciousness because we are moving our awareness away from the physical world to become more aware of ourselves as energy. Trance is a tool, and training the mind to become more passive and moving into a trance state allows the spirit world to influence the medium even more. In this altered state the medium has the potential to work with trance speaking, trance healing, trance communication and even trance art or music, all created in the trance state. It is a cooperation of spirit, where the mind of those in the spirit world takes control of the medium's faculties.

I have an interest in physical mediumship too. Physical mediumship phenomena can be seen and heard by every person in the room, whether those attending are mediumistic or not. Over many years I have had experiences that cannot be explained when I have sat in the altered state. I do not want to label this as physical mediumship; however, it is something I would like to explore more in the future.

I believe that every reading is special. Mediumship is about touching the soul, and if we can do that with the help of those in the spirit world then we are doing something quite magical. I love it when demonstrating, if a piece of very different evidence is given. One of the most bizarre readings I have done was when I was communicating with a man in spirit, who felt like a New Age/hippy character. He was talking about memories on a beach with friends, where he used to blow smoke rings. (This evidence was accepted by the recipient.) He then showed me him pulling party poppers with his teeth. (This was also accepted.) The spirit communicator then said he did of all this while balancing a bottle of beer on each hand! This evidence was understood too, and it gave me such a buzz to share his happy memory.

I am, in a way, looking forward to going to the spirit world when my time comes. I think the actual way that I will die is more of a worry to me regarding any potential pain and also the effect that my death will have on my family. But being in the spirit world is something to be excited about: finding out if it is as we imagined and experiencing the freedom we will have in that new life.

Medium and tutor
Age, 59
Crewe in Cheshire, in the North West of England

www.medium-lynnparker.co.uk
lynn.parker35@btopenworld.com

Chapter fourteen

JEFFREY PECK

Jeffrey and I met on a course at the college in 2019, where we were both students together with the wonderful English medium Chris Drew. Mediumship was very new to Jeffrey at the time, but regardless he had terrific abilities as a medium. On our first day together in the class we were asked to do a reading with a random partner who was completely blindfolded. I sat in front of Jeffrey, who couldn't see anything and had no idea who was before him. Immediately he connected with Sam, and I was amazed. Jeffrey talked of the car accident and the fact that Sam passed away with other people, which was correct. He described the very essence of Sam's personality, and Jeffrey also felt the deep love that Sam had for me. We both ended up in tears after the emotional intensity of the reading. I feel that Sam intentionally selected Jeffrey to be his 'chosen medium' for that reading, as it gave Jeffrey the much-needed confidence from all the accurate information he received. Jeffrey's abilities as a medium were truly confirmed, and it is for that reason that I too chose Jeffrey to be a contributor in this book. Jeffrey lives in San Francisco in the United States and now works full-time as a practising medium.

Since my first encounter with the spirit world at the age of thirty-eight, I have become well acquainted with a number of mediums from around the world, and as our friendships developed, we have shared our own experiences with one another. When I've talked to them about the beginning of their 'knowing', most seem to have countless and vivid stories and memories about seeing and hearing spirits from early childhood. Some have had experiences where the spirit world has been prominent and obvious to them since birth. I didn't have any experiences as a child with the spirit world – none whatsoever, absolutely nothing.

My early life was filled with parents, small-town experiences and confusion. I was born in 1970 in Fairbanks, Alaska, and my parents, Gloria and Bob, were living there because my father was a commissioned officer in the United States Army. My sister, Kristin, arrived in 1972, and not long afterwards Dad was to be sent to Vietnam, but the war ended abruptly in 1973, and his deployment was no longer necessary. Dad left the armed services after serving for four years, and our family returned home to South Dakota, where both of my parents had been born and raised. All of the extended family on both sides still resided there, and it seemed to be very important to my parents that we all stay together.

My father's job was managing the local department store in Brookings, South Dakota, where my mother worked as well in retail. I started high school in the town of Chamberlain, where I attended for only one year; then, sadly, my parents separated. I went with my dad to live in Phoenix, Arizona, while Kristin stayed with my mom in Chamberlain. It was a very difficult time in my life, and I only saw my mother and sister about twice a year.

Unfortunately, my father and I were never very close, but I had my reasons for wanting to remain living with him. After experiencing life in a bigger city, there was no way I could return to South Dakota, as the small-town mentality that existed there made it impossible for me to feel comfortable with knowing that I was gay. My father was incapable of being there emotionally for me because he was still in such turmoil over his marriage breakdown with Mom. We never had a great relationship as I was growing up, but we are now good friends.

In 1998 I completed high school in Phoenix, and afterwards I headed to Arizona State University in Tempe. I had no idea what I wanted to do with my life, and I attended university because most of my friends were going. Initially, I started a very general major, a liberal arts degree. I ended up dropping out because my heart just wasn't in it. I needed to support myself, and I got a job waiting tables in a local restaurant. It was a tough period in my life, and that time of confusion lasted for a while.

By age twenty-five, I was still confused in many ways, and I hadn't come out to my family as a gay man. The secret was mine alone, and it was playing havoc with me mentally. I had moved from Phoenix to Minneapolis in November 1994, because Minneapolis was still far enough away from South Dakota while having the cosmopolitan city close at hand. Looking back, I was attempting to run away from myself as I couldn't face the fact that I was gay. Like many gay men my age I felt shame, I felt wrong and I felt like a disappointment to myself and to my family. I had little or no sense of self-worth, and didn't feel I was of value to anybody, including myself. I not only hadn't come out to my parents, but I had also barely come out to myself. Yet by moving away, I had this misplaced notion in my head that I would meet a nice girl, we would somehow start dating and get married. Kids would follow, and I would live the quintessential suburban life of a straight man.

Of course, this was never going to be the case, and I had tried to 'pray the gay away' since I was in my early teens. After living in Minneapolis for three months, I realised that though I tried to run away from myself, I had followed 'me' there. There was no running anymore. I was in true despair with depression and anxiety and my wake-up call came one night at 1am when I was driving home from my waiting job during a dangerous blizzard. As I was trying to see while driving through the total whiteout, I was overwhelmed with tears in my heightened state of mental anguish. In the distance I could make out an electricity pole and I intentionally steered my car directly for it.

My mind was made up, and I wanted to end my life right then and there. No-one would ever need to know I was gay, and it would look like an accident. As all of these 'solutions' came to mind the strangest thing happened: I missed the electricity pole, and it felt like a hand literally came out of the sky and prevented my car from hitting the solid pole. Afterwards, I thought I must have hit a patch of ice that changed the direction of my car. Now I believe it was my guardian angels. The realisation of what I'd almost done struck me deeply, and it made me acknowledge that I had reached such a low point in my life. I had no self-esteem, self-love or self-worth, and this made me feel even more distressed.

Looking back, the experience allowed me to embrace self-acceptance of who I was, and it enabled me to 'come out of the closet' to my friends. I made phone call after phone call to the people who mattered in my life, and it was liberating. I wanted to tell my mother in person. She was now remarried to my stepfather, a wonderful man called Gary. Gary is the father of my half-brother, Josh, who is eighteen years younger than me.

Feeling empowered, I drove to South Dakota to see my family for Thanksgiving and, before I could say anything to Mom, she asked me if I was gay. So, I said yes. My mother then cried and prayed; this was her way of showing acceptance. In that moment and ever since, she never once made me feel unloved, dismissed or unseen. I chose not to tell my father I was gay until I was in my thirties, and since then there has been a lot of understanding and forgiveness between us both. Forgiveness, compassion and healing go a long way.

I floundered from job to job working mainly in hospitality, as it was something I could do easily and well. I genuinely like people, so working with the public suited my personality. In the mid-1990s, I went for an interview with the now defunct ATA Airlines, which flew charter flights internationally, and I was successful in getting a job as a flight attendant. I was twenty-seven, and this new and exciting career gave me a chance to see the world for the very first time. I loved my job, and my travel experiences were fantastic. The downside was that my income was so sparse I could barely support myself. After two fantastic years, I had no choice other than to leave and find a better-paying job.

Over the years my mother had become very unwell with chronic pain – fibromyalgia, a degenerative disc disease – and osteoarthritis had overtaken her body. I felt the need to do something personally to help her, so in 2006 I became attuned to reiki with hopes that it could help to alleviate my mom's pain, even for a little bit. I began my studies with a number of different reiki masters, and I thoroughly enjoyed all that I learnt over the next six years. As part of my initial reiki training at level one, my reiki master asked me to administer a reiki treatment every day for the next thirty days on myself. She emphasised, 'I want you to feel it. I want the reiki to teach you. I want you to experience it.' I did exactly as I was instructed, and every day I sat in my walk-in closet for an hour and gave myself a reiki treatment.

During those thirty days, I started to see a kaleidoscope of colours behind my eyelids, and I began to feel sensations I had never previously noticed. Everything was very new to me. I experienced 'seeing' (in my mind's eye) actual beings. I visualised what looked like vignettes, or little clips taken from movies, but these weren't movies I had ever seen before. Each day after finishing my self-treatment I knew that something really huge was happening, but at that moment I didn't know what it was.

I had no understanding of what was going on, so I told my reiki master about these unusual experiences. She returned with an all-knowing smile and said, 'You are opening up to spirit, and you are going to be a huge channel one day.' My only concept of a channel was what I'd read and seen about the well-known medium Esther Hicks and Abraham. I told her I couldn't be a channel. I might see colours, but I'm not a channel. My instructor said, 'Well then, you need to change your definition of the word channel.'

I began working part-time as a reiki practitioner and putting my new-found spiritual skills to use. In each reiki session I automatically started to psychically receive more and more information about the person I was working with. Each treatment and outcome was quite different, and I experienced clairvoyance, where I could 'see' places, things and people very clearly. I encountered the feeling of an unseen presence, which resulted in an incredibly peaceful healing for my clients and for me.

In the very early years of practising my reiki, a friend asked me to see a woman called Louise, who had been quite ill for many years. My friend didn't give me any details about her illness, as they knew I preferred to work that way. Prior to treating Louise, I silently went into a meditation and concentrated on her health issues. While in prayer, I asked for assistance and support from my guides and guardians. I asked heaven what I needed to know about Louise. I was told she had five discordant energies. From my reiki training, I knew that every thought produces a 'form', which becomes a part of the collective consciousness. This form can be maintained for a long or short period of time, depending on the amount of energy attached to it. It is these discordant thoughts that may create blockages within the body, possibly leading to illness, internal turmoil and conflict.

The answer I received during my meditation was that Louise was struggling with overwhelming feelings of hate, guilt, anger, doubt and the hatred of men specifically. Even though I had complete faith in the powerful effect of reiki and the importance of gaining clarity through meditation, I was immediately sceptical because I felt that the first four emotions could apply to any one of us, at any given time. However, the last one, hatred of men... that was very specific.

I met Louise at her home, and as I was preparing to start the treatment she began to describe her ailments to me. During the previous year she almost died, and since then she had been relying on ten major life-saving medications each day. I assisted Louise in getting up onto the table, and she quickly relaxed to the soothing background music. Frequently, I was honoured to have the presence of Jesus in my treatments. With my eyes closed I could 'see' the room, as if I had my eyes wide open. There was an unforgettable glow about it, and I could see this room filled with angelic beings. It was the first time I had ever experienced such clarity. Yet my inner sceptic was trying to logically override this surreal and wonderful experience. It felt like a childlike dream that could only be happening in my own imagination. I felt a change in the air pressure around me, and I saw Jesus standing on the other side of the table with his hands over Louise's feet and ankles. The brightest white light was coming from his hands.

During the entire session my own eyes were closed, yet I was seeing Louise's body very clearly, and I was able to witness the dark particles of energy departing from seven different places in her body. The reiki was working! It was clearing out the negative energies, and it was amazing to see. I was beside myself with joy, and again that little sceptic in the back of my head rolled his eyes, as if to suggest I was having some sort of mental episode.

Afterwards Louise just lay there, almost as if she was intoxicated. There was a softness in the way she looked that had not been present before, and I helped her up very slowly. She sat there in a daze and just stared at the floor. Louise said, 'I never knew. I never knew ... that one could experience such peace. I just never knew.' Louise then she reached up with a gesture to hug me, and she whispered in my ear, 'I saw black tornadoes coming out of my body.' When she said this, my knees almost buckled and I nearly went straight down to the floor. I was amazed by what she said, but I didn't react openly to it. I answered quite calmly, 'Yes, the energy was clearing you, and you were healing. Isn't it beautiful.' Then she continued, 'I saw angels all around us in this room. I saw Christ standing at my feet.'

I got in my car, and no sooner did the door close than I started sobbing. I was in such a state of gratitude and heavenly awe that I couldn't even turn the car's ignition on for about five minutes. It wasn't for me to know specifically what had happened in Louise's past lifetime that had caused her to have those deeply felt negative emotions of hate, guilt, anger, doubt and hatred of men. But I was elated I could remove these negative emotions for her.

My ongoing reiki sessions with my mother helped alleviate her chronic pain, and Mom was amazed by how much it improved her quality of life. Previously, my mother was only respectful of Western medicine and prayer; nothing New Age at all was acceptable to her. It was a wonderful feeling to know I could help my mother in some way, and I had many other people coming to me for reiki treatments. At this time I was living back in Phoenix, and I ran my successful little reiki business on a part-time basis.

My main source of income was working privately in the residential mortgage business, where I handled and provided loans for homebuyers. After leaving the airline, I gained finance experience as a loans officer in a local bank in Phoenix, where I worked for two years. I made the decision to take the knowledge that I had acquired at the bank and move into the real estate world. My business grew quickly, and I was very successful; however, this all changed in 2008 when the global financial crisis hit and, like millions of people worldwide, I lost everything. It killed my business overnight. I lost my home to foreclosure, my car was repossessed, I had to file for bankruptcy and coincidentally the ten-year relationship that I was in also abruptly ended. All. At. Once. My life was truly in shreds, and I had nothing to show for all of my hard work, both privately and professionally.

In order to escape everything I flew to Maui in Hawaii and stayed with good friends, who were a huge support to me. Because of my reiki training I was at least able to resume working in some capacity, and my first experience with mediumship happened while I was in Hawaii. I was giving a client a treatment, and I felt the presence of someone else in the room. I wasn't worried by this in any way, and I intuitively knew the man's grandfather was with me. I was able to describe his grandfather's personality, and I felt his very essence. It was a moving experience, and it felt very natural in how it all unfolded. The grandfather in spirit showed me a huge apple tree; I could see it clearly, and there was a sense of pride about the tree that I felt from him. After the treatment my client told me that his grandfather was well known in the area for having this massive apple tree in his backyard, and it was his pride and joy. We were both astonished by what had just happened. The reading was spontaneous, and it wasn't intentional at all on my part.

With other clients I also began to inadvertently make these connections with spirit as I was doing reiki treatments on them. I was always very careful about what I said, or didn't say, to the person, because I didn't want to frighten anyone. I guess I used my own intuition about how much or how little I shared with them. At first I really didn't understand what was happening with these spirit communications I was having, but I did know with certainty I wanted to explore them further.

While I was still staying in Hawaii, Doreen Virtue, a well-known New Age teacher at the time, was running a one-week workshop in Maui, and I knew I had to attend. There were two hundred and fifty students at the workshop, and each day we were divided into smaller groups, in which we did psychic readings for one another using Doreen's own brand of Angel cards. I found I could read the cards very naturally, and a story would just unfold that was always verified as accurate. After the course I felt I was meant to work in the spiritual field, so I created a small website and started doing paid psychic card readings with my newly acquired Tarot and Angel cards. This was all fine, and I really enjoyed the readings, but in terms of being a financially viable new career path, it wasn't paying the bills.

I returned to Phoenix in 2011, where I met a new partner. We soon decided to move in together. My financial situation had not improved much since the GFC, and I asked the universe for guidance and direction to help me with my life. I shouted to heaven, 'I will do whatever I need to do for you, but I will not do it broke!' Within a month, I secured a new job as the personal assistant to a very wealthy older couple, who lived for half of the year in Scottsdale, an upmarket suburb in Arizona, and the other half in the Bay Area of San Francisco. The couple made their wealth from various businesses in Silicon Valley, and they lived a very rich and privileged lifestyle in their retirement. This was like a dream come true for my partner and I, and it meant that we travelled year-round with the couple and lived independently in beautiful accommodation nearby.

My relationship with my new employers was a tricky one. I really liked the husband; we always got along very well, and there was a strong mutual respect between us. However, his wife was a very difficult person to work for. Though my role was demanding, I enjoyed it immensely at first, but I wasn't expecting to be on-call twenty-four-seven with little to no annual leave. My job was all-encompassing: I was the chauffeur, cook, sorted the laundry and dry-cleaning. I also did the shopping and ran all their errands. Behind the scenes, I managed the payment of all the household accounts, booked their travel, and I scheduled and drove them both to their medical appointments. Thankfully, my job was very financially lucrative, and our housing was also provided, so this made it tolerable.

In January 2015, I married my partner of five years. Throughout that year I became highly aware of all things spiritual, and I started reading lots of books and listening to dozens of spiritual podcasts and radio shows. Mediumship seemed to be everywhere on television and in the movies too, and I began to feel an unexplained calling within to do something about it. I listened to yet another podcast about mediumship, and the presenter was talking about a place in England called the Arthur Findlay College, and I knew that I would be going there. I was also very aware that I couldn't go anywhere at all for a long while, because at the time I was still working for the couple, and I wasn't given any personal time off. Later on during my employment the husband sadly passed away, and staying on with his widow was unworkable, so I left.

As soon as I resigned from my PA role, I made reservations to attend two weeks of courses starting in July 2019. Up until March of 2019 I hadn't ever intentionally performed a mediumship reading for anyone. My contact with the spirit world had only ever occurred quite naturally and spontaneously while I was treating some of my reiki clients in the past. Prior to going to the United Kingdom in the July, I felt I should get some hands-on mediumship training closer to home, so I found a medium online called Colby Rebel in Los Angeles, and I began my training with her. It all went well, and very soon Colby had me doing practice readings with volunteers via Zoom. These were both mediumship and psychic sittings, and I loved doing them.

I was quite surprised when Colby told me she had a platform demonstration workshop coming up on the first of June, and she felt that I was ready to push myself and participate. Colby could have been speaking in another language, because I didn't understand what demonstrating was. I knew it required me to stand up and speak before an audience, which was nerve-wracking enough, but when I learnt that I was also expected to deliver messages from spirit, I felt paralysed with fear.

I knew this opportunity was being put in my path for a reason, so following what I knew to be right, I booked into Colby's platform demonstrating course. After arriving for my first class, we were told that all of us had to do a platform demonstration in front of a small crowd that night. I was honestly quite shocked, as I had never done anything like that before and because my spiritual development was still in its infancy. I hadn't ever done a proper mediumship reading in person either; everything to date had been done remotely on Zoom.

During the day all ten of us students had two practice runs for the demonstration that was to take place later that evening. I knew I had to go through with my first experience on the platform, and in spite of my fear I really wanted to succeed. While waiting for my turn I honestly thought I was going to faint, and I was more terrified about the public speaking aspect of the reading than actually making contact with a spirit communicator. It was very daunting to have twenty-eight enthusiastic guests present, who were all eagerly wanting to hear messages from their loved ones in spirit. Thankfully, my platform demonstration went really well.

Finally, my trip and two weeks of study at Arthur Findlay College arrived, and I flew to London. Other than my mediumship workshop with Colby a few months earlier, I had never done any other training, with the exception of my Doreen Virtue course in Hawaii. I put complete trust in heaven, and I asked to be put wherever I needed to be, in terms of my class level at the college.

Chris Drew, the course coordinator, interviewed everyone briefly on arrival and asked us privately where we thought we should be placed in relation to our level of experience. I told Chris of my very limited experience of only four months of formal mediumship development. I had no preconceived ideas about which class I would be in, and I instinctively knew I would be placed exactly where I needed to be. The amazing thing was that I ended up in Chris's class, which was the advanced group, and he introduced me to the other students as the 'water baby'. Water babies instinctively know how to swim, and I instinctively knew how to communicate with spirit. It was synchronicity after synchronicity with everything that happened that week. I was able to participate properly in all of the class readings, including the one-on-one sittings and the platform demonstrations. I was elated.

Prior to my going to the college, my husband was very encouraging, and he supported me emotionally in pursuing my wish to develop my mediumship. Unbeknown to me, he also expected I would attend my two weeks of study at the college, come home and instantly start earning a lucrative income working full-time as a medium. When he told me this I was absolutely dumbfounded because this was my own personal spiritual journey; it wasn't some money-making scheme for our future wealth. A combination of issues led to us divorcing in 2020.

I was raised in the Lutheran church, and I always believed in the afterlife; it was a 'knowing' to me. We attended church most Sundays, and for Easter and Christmas, but we weren't what I would call a super religious family. When I was a teenager and starting to grow into myself, I instinctively knew I was different in some way, and I soon realised that it was because I was gay. I always believed there was something else after death, but I had also been conditioned by the Church to just believe in heaven and hell, and for me, it was all very traumatic because as a gay man, hell was where I would be going.

My mother is now an extremely devout member of the Wesleyan church, and regardless she is very supportive of my mediumship, for which I am grateful. Mom doesn't quite understand it, but she does still fully support me and my experiences. She likes to hear about my readings, but I think she has a hard time reconciling my experiences with her own religious beliefs, as my stories are so foreign to her. However, my mom does believe what I experience with my mediumship to be very real.

My maternal grandmother passed in 2002, and since then she has communicated with me on many occasions. We were very close, and my wonderful relationship with her has continued to grow since she passed. I know she is helping me with my mediumship, and I feel I can talk to her very openly and ask her for guidance whenever I need it. She was present during my weeks at Arthur Findlay, and I loved how she came through often during the practice readings with my fellow students. I told Mom about my communications with my grandmother, but I'm still not sure she is able to process what it all really means. It's almost too abstract for her to grasp. Mom says, 'If she's in heaven with Jesus, how can she be talking to you?' Mom is trying to process everything logically, and understanding mediumship definitely doesn't work in that way.

I feel I travelled through the first forty-odd years of my life without any real direction until I found what was always there waiting for me, my untapped mediumship abilities. Now I know that my life's purpose is to work with spirit and to offer communication, comfort and healing to all those who come to me for a reading. In 2017, I lost a very close friend called Lucas in a tragic accident. Since then I have had a lot of contact with him in spirit, which has been very comforting to me and for his family. Knowing that Lucas is constantly around me brings me peace, and I know that he will help me in any way he can from the other side.

As far as platform demonstrations go, I feel that in time and after further practical hands-on learning and experience, I will do private and public demonstrations outside of the Spiritualist churches. Spiritualist churches are not generally common throughout America, which is so different to the United Kingdom, where they are in plentiful supply. By the grace of spirit, mediumship has become my sole source of income since my divorce.

Life has never been better, more complete and more aligned with my purpose and my soul. I have faith, hope and trust in spirit, and I know I am exactly where I am meant to be.

Medium
Age, 51
San Francisco, CA, USA

www.jeffreypeck.com
jeffrey.j.peck@gmail.com

Chapter fifteen

ANGIE MORRIS

Angie was one of my tutors when I attended the college in early 2017. Each week at the college all students are able to book and pay for a one-on-one mediumship reading or a spiritual assessment. The latter is where the tutor does a reading based on what they 'see' in our abilities as mediums. With this type of reading there is no connection to the spirit world involved, it's done on a psychic level and that was what I opted to have.

Prior to the trip I had decided to write a book about Sam's passing and what happened thereafter for us as a family. It was always going to be a book of hope, but I had no idea about where to start or what to say. I took a blank exercise book away with me, as I intended to start writing my manuscript while I was at the college. During my reading Angie told me I would be writing a book! I then felt Sam's spiritual presence; I didn't say a word to Angie, but I knew that Sam was so excited by what Angie was saying about the impending book. Angie then stopped and said, 'Kerry, this is not supposed to be a mediumship reading, but I have your son here!' I told her that I was very aware of Sam's presence too, and she confirmed that he was so happy about the book being written.

I had all the confirmation I needed, and when I arrived back home in Australia, I went into the city and bought a new laptop and started writing my book, which was released in 2018. I was able to present Angie with her own copy when I ran into her unexpectedly on another course the following year. Angie is a very gifted medium, who is funny and kind, and I'm thrilled she was prepared to be a part of this next book. Angie lives in the United Kingdom and works professionally as a medium and tutor at Arthur Findlay College.

As a four-year-old I played very easily and happily with my younger brother, Rob, who was two and a half. Words were unnecessary between us because I was innocently and inadvertently tuning into

Rob's thoughts, so he never used his own voice or spoke at all. I knew what he wanted, and I would get it for him. This meant that Rob never felt the need to communicate verbally with anyone. I was completely fine with this, but our parents were not. Rob's delayed speech was a real concern for them, and they knew that my constant telepathic indulgences weren't helping, so we were separated until Rob found his own voice and finally grasped spoken language for himself.

I am one of four children, and I come second in line after Shirley, then Rob and lastly Richard, who we all call Rit. My parents, Ann and Syd, are both retired, and they ran pubs earlier on. At one stage they had two of them, one in Ipswich and another in Peterborough in the United Kingdom. Family life was very hectic in the hotels, and they later decided to seek work in different jobs: Mum went back to nursing, and my father took up driving lorries in the local area.

When I was young I had some very strange experiences I couldn't understand, let alone explain. At night when I was in bed, the furniture used to move and tap about on its own accord, and though I found this to be quite frightening I didn't share this phenomena with anyone else in the family, and it remained my secret. Many years later, I thought I heard my grandfather's voice speaking to me, and I kept looking to find him, but I saw nothing. What I didn't know was at that exact same time my maternal grandfather had passed away suddenly. This was my first encounter with a spirit communicator, and back then I had no understanding or concept about mediums or mediumship. To me, I was just having a very strange experience.

Afterwards my grandfather kept communicating with me constantly, and just before I went to sleep most nights he would tap me on the shoulder and I would nervously hide under the duvet. I could smell the brand of his cigarettes in my bedroom. I knew he was there with me, and it was more confusing than comforting. When my great-grandmother died I was only twelve years old, and just like with my grandfather I could communicate with her as well. I wasn't sure what was happening with either connection. I didn't understand it, but regardless it was very real. No-one in our family ever talked about such things, so neither did I.

When I was sixteen, I was living in an adolescent care facility in Norwich, which was run by Social Services, and I was there of my own choosing. Everyone living at the centre was aged between sixteen and eighteen years. We had social workers living with us full-time, and we were in their care. It was only me at this place; none of my siblings were with me. After leaving school, I completed a youth training scheme, and I managed to get a job at one of the offices in the County Hall. I was paid twenty-seven pounds per week, and I was grateful to have any job at all, as work was scarce at the time.

I moved around a lot in these early years, so I never really put down roots long enough to make and develop many close friendships. I had my daughter, Gemma, when I was seventeen, and I brought her into this world on my own, and alone. Some years later, I got married, and even though this union didn't last, we did produce a son called Sam. After my first marriage broke down and we separated, Gemma, Sam and I moved to Norfolk to live with my parents. Prior to my separation, I was working very happily as a medical secretary in Ipswich, where we had all lived. Initially, I did the one-hour commute each way by car from Norfolk to Ipswich, but all the travelling, working full-time and being there for my young family all proved to be too hard, so I felt I had to resign from my job. Luckily, I found a new position in a health centre, where I worked as a secretary.

When we first moved back to Norfolk, my mother was constantly talking to me about some Spiritualist church that she wanted to visit, and I kept thinking that I really didn't want to go to any blooming church! One Sunday, I was feeling a bit bored so I decided to take Mum to this church, as I knew she was very keen to go. I was twenty-nine years old at the time, newly divorced, and I had absolutely no clue what happened in a Spiritualist church. As the service began Mum was very excited about everything. It all seemed pleasant enough, but I had no idea what to expect.

We both sat at the back of the church, and the woman who was addressing the congregation was giving an uplifting prayer. The service then became very different to anything I had previously experienced, and the same woman started to make some sort of connection with someone in the spirit world. I was sitting very low in the pew as I really didn't want this woman, who I later realised was a medium, to come to me. Even though I was nervous about the whole service and these strange spirit communications, I was very intrigued by what I had just witnessed.

As we left the church I noticed a sign advertising an open day for the next week, so I decided to go along to see what it was all about. That day I had a one-on-one reading with a medium for the very first time in my life. The medium told me so many things about my life and about myself. These were things I had never spoken to anyone else about, and yet she knew so much about me and my past. The medium then brought my great-grandmother through and shared wonderful evidence of her survival into the spirit world, which I found astounding. This same medium also told me I would go to a college called Arthur Findlay to study mediumship myself. Obviously, I had never heard of the place.

The session was being recorded by the medium on a tape recorder, and at the start she played a bit of the reading back to make sure the tape was working and recording properly. The sitting was remarkable, and when I tried to replay the tape at home, it was totally blank and had recorded nothing that was said. It was almost like the medium had given me too much information all at once and I wouldn't be able to deal with it all. She had also told me to join a spiritual development group and a mediumship circle, neither of which I understood; but I obediently joined one of each.

The church ran the mediumship circle group, and on my first visit I was able to make connections with spirit immediately, and these communications were visually as clear to me as seeing a living person. I had been sitting in my circle for only eighteen months when the medium running the class became very sick and she asked me to take over temporarily so that the classes could continue. The only issue was that she never returned, and I was left teaching all the other students each week. My spiritual development classes didn't go nearly as smoothly for me as my mediumship classes. In the various exercises we did I could never see any colours or tune in with the energy of a living person, but if I was working with the spirit world, I had no trouble at all in connecting. I found doing the psychic readings for living people way more challenging than communicating with the dead.

I later attended my first mediumship awareness course, which was run by a wonderful medium called Simone Key. Simone was such a good teacher, and she gave me so much support and confidence in going forward with my own mediumship. During this time I would randomly go into the various Spiritualist churches nearby to watch the different mediums working and to see how they did things. I had positive experiences with witnessing some amazing readings, but not always. It was a great way to learn through observing others in a non-judgemental way.

Simone invited me to go with her to the many Spiritualist churches in the surrounding area, and I said yes. Simone conducted lots of the church services and did the mediumship demonstration as well. She was very highly regarded in her work and rightly so. One week we were at Bury St Edmunds Spiritualist Church in Suffolk, and I was sitting at the back waiting for the service to begin. The church protocol is that the officiate and the medium conducting the service wait outside until everyone is seated, and then they enter from the rear of the church and take their places at the front. On one particular week, as Simone and the chairperson entered, Simone grabbed me and pulled me up saying, 'You're going to do a message tonight.' I honestly felt I was about to throw up, as I had never done a platform demonstration before in front of an audience.

Previously, I had only practised demonstrating after the Sunday service, and even though I had made contact with spirits at those sessions I was just practising with the other new mediums. Us students were all learning how to use our abilities properly in a classroom situation, and being in front of a live and real congregation of parishioners was completely new to me. I was terrified.

Simone gave me no choice, so at the appropriate time I went to the platform and I started the communication. The spirit communicator came through, and I went off like a machine gun. I was speaking so quickly and blurting out all this information, and then I promptly sat down. The reading was for a man present in the congregation, and it all went very well, regardless of the rapid speed in which I spoke. After I finished Simone said, 'That was rather quick. Would you like to do another one?' I declined, but I felt very privileged afterwards to be asked by Simone to do another contact, as it showed that she believed in me and my capabilities. Now I needed to have the same self-belief.

None of my mediumship unfoldment was what I wanted personally; it just happened for me and I hadn't been actively pursuing it, as I know that many people do. I continued going to various churches around the area with Simone, and she kept getting me up to do the mediumship demonstrations. I really started to enjoy the experience. After one particular service, Simone was asked by a committee member if she had her diary with her so she could be booked to be the medium at another date. Simone answered, 'No, but Angie takes bookings!' At that stage I had never given an inspirational prayer (or an opening or closing one either), and

I'd never given an address to the congregation or done an entire mediumship demonstration on my own. I felt I had no choice as I didn't want to let Simone down, so I took the booking to do the entire service on my own.

At the time I was sitting in a mediumship development circle at Simone's home, and she would often try out many varying ways of teaching us students. Simone would have us practising lots of different things, and the culmination of what she taught us allowed me the confidence to complete my first solo church service. I felt reasonably confident with my mediumship, but like most people I felt I couldn't speak confidently in public at all. On the day of my first address, I took along my 'ghetto blaster' to the church, and I soon realised there were no power points in the right places for me to plug it in. Eventually, we got it working with batteries, and I played some uplifting music from Westlife, who were a huge boy band at the time. They were all upbeat songs that were meant to energise the congregation and to give me the inspiration I needed to give my prayer, address and finally give the mediumship demonstration.

In the Spiritualist churches, when giving the addresses we don't use any written notes from a previously scripted talk; we speak spontaneously about something relevant that inspires us at that moment. Everything thankfully went to plan, and this was the first of many future church addresses I participated in.

It was during my time attending the circle at the church that I met my future husband, Craig, who is a medium too. After the Sunday services we both began doing the practice demonstrations that were designed to prepare us newly trained mediums to work with in the Spiritualist churches. Craig decided early on that demonstrating wasn't for him; he preferred to do healing work, and this was something he continued to do for quite a long time. Eventually, Craig's work took up more and more time, and he finally decided to pull away from doing any further healing work in the Church. We married sixteen years ago in the same Spiritualist church that we met in. I call Craig a lazy medium in jest, as he has the ability but he chooses not to use it.

Simone told me about a college where she taught on a regular basis, called Arthur Findlay College. This was the same college that the original medium had predicted I would attend when I had my first one-on-one reading. Craig had already been to do a few courses at the college, and he knew all about it. We have since gone together a few times. It was just after my thirtieth birthday that I went to the college for the very first time on my own. I was very timid and quite reserved at first, but I gained confidence after other students and tutors asked why I wasn't working as a medium outside of the churches already. After that I started going to lots of courses at the college.

I was asked to be a student helper at the college, during a course called 'Willing to Work', which is the trainee tutors' course. I was there as a student only; my role was to be a volunteer for the trainee tutors if they needed one in a class situation. During one of these sessions, I was asked to look at some spiritual cards and 'go into the power' and then do a spontaneous address to show the class what was expected of them when giving an address to a church congregation. There was a tutor present called Eamon Downey, and he was assessing the trainee tutors I was volunteering for. Eamon saw my address, and he invited me to do the teachers' training program at the college to become a tutor there myself. I joked that I didn't feel I was ready to do so, and nothing more was said.

I later applied to do another course at the college and filled in a pile of forms, assuming I was applying for a week-long mediumship course. I didn't realise that the forms were for teacher training, just as Eamon Downey had recommended to me some time earlier. Simone Key was heading the committee for all the new trainee tutors, and she commented to me that it was great that I had applied. I then explained it was a mistake; nevertheless, I agreed to start the three-year teaching training program at Arthur Findlay College.

I was still in my early thirties when I began training as a tutor, and I found the whole process to be quite difficult because so many of the older tutors had very strong opinions about me being there. Some said I was too young, or they felt I hadn't been doing mediumship for long enough, or I hadn't sat in circle for the right amount of time, and many also felt that I hadn't worked the platform enough to have the necessary experience to teach the students. At times, you needed to have a hard shell just to survive and to cope with all of the nastiness. These negative reactions were all ego driven and very human, but we as mediums are supposed to work in a more cohesive way. Sadly, it doesn't always happen that way. Regardless, I kept going, completed my tutor training and became qualified to teach at the college.

I had left school quite early, and this always played on my mind, as it impacted on my ability to do any further study as an adult. I decided to complete my A Levels and began a counselling degree at university, hoping to work with victims of crime. Unfortunately, it wasn't what I had hoped for, and I didn't continue with my degree. During this time I was also working as a volunteer at Victims Support, an independent charity, and I ended up being offered a full-time job with them in a very well-paid position, which I absolutely loved.

Prior to starting my teacher training program at Arthur Findlay, I was already working at the college in a paid position doing private mediumship sittings every Tuesday for the outside community. I became the resident medium (even though I didn't live-in), and I did this for eighteen years on a regular basis. To become the resident medium, I gave up my wonderful full-time job in Victims Support to work for just one day a week doing the private sittings. Thankfully, over time, my hours of work increased.

In early 2019, I felt completely burnt out with my mediumship and my lack of work-life balance. I was forever packing and unpacking my suitcase to teach for a week or more at a time the college and I were totally exhausted. Craig knew that something was amiss when I burst into tears and said, 'I don't want to go back.' I made a very difficult phone call to the college and cancelled the next two weeks of teaching immediately. I felt very guilty about pulling the pin so late, but I just couldn't do it. I started to learn a lot about Angie over those two weeks, and I knew I was totally burnt out; there was nothing left of me at all, mentally, physically, spiritually … nothing! I told the college I was taking a few months off teaching, and they were very understanding. I cancelled all my commitments for the rest of 2019.

I undertook a course as a teaching assistant for children in infant schools, and I achieved my Higher Level Advanced Certificate. I then did further study, which allowed me to work with children with learning difficulties. This was very satisfying, and I was proud of myself; however, gaining work in this field seemed impossible. Craig and I sold our home, and we moved to Norwich, where I got a short-lived job working in a department store, which I absolutely hated. I kept receiving emails from people asking me to do private sittings for them, and I decided that doing just one reading wouldn't hurt. Once I started, I had calls and emails from so many unknown people wanting private sittings. I wasn't actively looking for the bookings; they just constantly came to me.

Alyson Gannon, a medium and friend from the United States, emailed me asking if I would teach online with her and my old friend Sharon Harvey, from the college. I had missed my teaching and mediumship work, so I agreed to join them, and I resigned from the department store. I was very fortunate to already be working online with my students as Covid-19 hit the following year and everything changed worldwide. I am now also back teaching at the college, albeit via Zoom, as in-person classes have ceased since March 2020. It's great to be back, and I'm doing what I love. I just needed to find the right balance in my working life.

Growing up I went to Church of England schools that always had a church service to start the day, but that was the sum total of my religious guidance. My parents were not religious, and no-one went to church outside of the compulsory school attendances. For the past twenty plus years, I have been a member of the Spiritualist Church, but this doesn't mean you must attend church regularly or not have an alcoholic drink or smoke a cigarette. Spiritualists do silly things and everyday normal stuff just like everybody else; it is not a strict religious discipline. History tells us that mediumship was once carried out by the priests, who would commune directly and openly with spirits during a church service. This aspect of the service in non-Spiritualist churches is long gone, and it's now sadly viewed as a form of devil worship, which is a real misconception that causes so much unwarranted fear.

Death is a very natural process. It's the next step after life, and if we could teach everyone from a very early age that death happens to everything, then many of the misconceptions would not exist. I believe we should begin by teaching children about the life cycle of plants and flowers and how they all start out young and small, they blossom into full life and then they die. It's life's cycle, and it happens to humans and animals as well. If we adopted this more natural approach to explaining it, then maybe things might be clearer and different in how life and death is understood.

Over the years I've experienced many wonderful readings, and the most amazing one was during a private sitting at the college during Open Week. A male spirit communicator came through for his wife who was having the reading. I kept hearing three words from her husband: 'The cancer's gone.' I knew that ethically I couldn't tell her this, but it was so clear and he wouldn't stop saying it; he was desperate for me to share this message with his wife. I felt I had no other option, so I repeated these three words to her. The woman simply replied 'Thank you for that' and then she left; the reading was over.

A year later the same woman came back on another Open Week, and at first I didn't recognise her; she looked very different to the year before. She wanted to have another reading with me, and once again her husband came through, and the first thing she said was, 'Say to him, he was absolutely right by the way – it's gone.' The genuine love, strength and power of this communication has stayed with me always.

At another lovely sitting, a female spirit came to me before her funeral had even taken place. The spirit communicator was describing everything in detail that her family were planning to do at her upcoming funeral service, and she was saying, 'I don't want this, and can you change that to this?' Her family members, who I was doing the reading for, sat there looking utterly shocked. My spirit communicator also wanted changes made to parts of the eulogy, as it made her sound a bit boring and she wanted it spiced up a bit. It wasn't so much about their choice of flowers or music; it was more about properly reflecting her personality, and she wanted everyone at her funeral to understand who she was, and what she was really like when she lived.

I've found over the years that the most reluctant students often make the best mediums. It's these students, who often doubt their natural mediumistic abilities and aren't desperate to become mediums, who generally thrive in their development. Their ego is firmly in check, and they have nothing to prove. I find it very difficult when a student says 'I want to be a medium' and they race ahead attending courses and workshops endlessly, perhaps lacking what it takes to become a medium.

My role as a medium has taken me to many places, and so far I've worked in Switzerland, Germany, The Netherlands, the Shetland Islands and in Austria, where I once did a demonstration in a castle. These wonderful trips have been a combination of demonstrations, private sittings and teaching. Some are for a week at a time, and I do these trips on my own. Most of my international work has come about via the students who have been in my group at the college, and they engage my services privately and arrange for me to work in their country. I love these opportunities to travel and work abroad with my mediumship, and I hope to do more in the future.

My own journey in life has made me much stronger and more confident as a person. I won't stand for any injustice, and I refuse to tolerate people being disrespectful of others. I will and do speak up to be the voice for those who can't stand up for themselves, and over the years this has got me in trouble many times. I honestly don't care if my stance upsets some people. My mediumship has changed me. I'm no longer frightened of others, or what they think of me. I'm completely happy being by myself, and I feel I don't have to try to prove anything to anyone any longer. I feel I have a voice now, and my voice is just as important as anybody else's. And for the first time in my entire life, I feel I have found something I'm good at, and I love it. Mediumship fits right with me.

Medium and tutor
Age, 52
Norwich, United Kingdom

www.angiejmorris.com
angiejmorris@me.com

 Chapter sixteen

Sharon Harvey

I met Sharon in early 2017 when I attended a course that she and Angie Morris were running at the college. I was privileged that week to witness a demonstration of physical mediumship that Sharon gave. It was an amazing experience, and I feel so fortunate to have been present with a small number of selected students. I also had a private mediumship sitting with Sharon that week, and both Sam and my father came through to communicate with me. Sharon gave a wonderful and very accurate reading, and she mentioned that I would be writing a book and there would be more than one of them. It seems only fitting that Sharon should now be a part of that second foreseen book. Sharon is delightful, with a wicked sense of humour. She is an English medium who works both privately and as a tutor at the college.

My mother said I was always talking to someone in my bedroom, but when she went in to check there was never anyone else in there. To be honest I don't really remember doing this, so I'm not sure who I was talking to. I can only assume that it was the spirit world. I do, however, clearly recall that when I was eight years old, I used to spend loads of time in our little spare bedroom making clothes for myself and my dolls on an old sewing machine. My mother could barely sew a button on, so the sewing machine wasn't something she used at all. No-one had ever shown me how to use the sewing machine; it was all totally instinctive, and I just knew exactly what to do.

I was born and raised in Enfield, North London, where my mother, Irene, was also born. My father, Algae Buckley, was a gypsy, and he was named after his father, another Algae, which is what families did back then. I have one older sister, and in keeping with family tradition she was named after my mother; sadly, Irene has since passed. My parents' marriage was not a happy one, and I was about four years old when they separated, so I have very few childhood memories of my father at all.

As a young man my father would do anything at all to make money. He used to collect scrap iron and metal to sell, and he was very handy and able to fix cars, but he wasn't a trained mechanic. When he was still a child, he would go door to door selling wax flowers in baskets, which were made of willow and moss, that my grandmother created. Dad and his family would purposely target the large mansions in wealthy London suburbs because they knew the people living there would buy whatever they were selling, because all were afraid that the gypsies would curse them if they didn't buy anything. After my parents divorced, Mum didn't ever remarry, so things were financially tough for her, battling away and raising her two daughters on her own. My mother worked as a cleaner in the large London homes, and she used to take Irene and me along with her when she worked, so she could still look after us.

Even though I didn't have a close relationship with my father, I did have a wonderful bond with his mother, Susan, who everyone knew as Susie, but I always called her little Nan. Years before my arrival into the world my paternal grandparents, Susie and Algae senior, were travelling gypsies who lived in a traditional horse-drawn gypsy caravan with their children. I have photos of them all including my father standing beside the caravan with my grandparents, who were both fiercely proud to come from gypsy stock.

My grandparents had twin girls, as well as my father and also other siblings. The twins were totally devoted to one another and quite inseparable. As the family travelled around the countryside the girls would build little fairy gardens at the camp sites, as part of their make-believe games. At every camp site there was always an open fire burning for cooking purposes and general warmth. One of the twins accidently put her hairbrush into the flames and somehow it exploded and burnt her body so badly that she died. Her sister was absolutely inconsolable, and she also died, presumably from a broken heart after losing her twin. They were both only around nine years old when this tragedy happened. The twins were both laid to rest together in the Edmonton Cemetery in North London, and my grandmother announced she wouldn't be travelling any longer, as she wanted to put down roots to be near her two girls.

My grandparents bought a house with a shop attached in North London, and this was how my grandmother made money to help support her family. Little Nan sold a huge range of things, including the handmade moss and willow baskets with the wax-covered flowers that my father used to sell as a boy. My grandparents were a very streetwise and industrious family, and at Christmas time they sold Christmas trees from the yard at the back of the house. My grandfather, Algae, was a very good psychic, as many gypsies are, and he made his money by gambling on the horse races. He intuitively always knew who was going to win, and he betted accordingly. I was eight or nine years old at the time, and I can remember my grandfather regularly winning four or five hundred pounds from his betting, a huge amount of money by today's standards and an enormous sum back then.

As a child I spent a lot of time at my grandparents' house, and I loved being there. Little Nan was a natural healer, and if she saw boys stealing birds' eggs from the nests, she would take the eggs from them, and somehow she knew how to keep them warm and at the right temperature, so that the eggs would eventually hatch. She then hand raised the chicks until they could survive on their own. Little Nan helped people too, and my mother once told me a story about my grandmother noticing a young boy who kept hiding his face in his mother's skirts. She saw that the child had horrible red boils all over his face, so she asked his mother to bring him to see her, adding that she could help him. The woman said they had been to see so many doctors since his birth, and no-one could help. Eventually, the mother took her son to see my grandmother, who applied natural potions she made from fresh herbs, and the young boy was healed completely.

I went to a government primary school in Enfield, and there was a Christian church club that was affiliated with the school; it was here that my interest in religion began. There was no religion at all in my home when I was growing up. When I was nine years old I was obsessed with Jesus, and it made me feel good to think about him and God. I began going to the local Church of England church by myself, and I would sit in the church for as long as possible, so I could experience this lovely feeling of belonging.

At fifteen I left Enfield High School to find employment anywhere I could. There was plenty of menial work around, and my first job was working at a factory that manufactured television parts. I didn't like the job at all, so I didn't stay long. Back then you could leave a job in the morning and get a brand-new one in the afternoon. I later worked at other factories, and every single place of employment left me feeling totally unsatisfied and unfulfilled, so I kept on moving jobs and getting another one.

Around this time I met my first husband, Paul, who was my girlfriend's older brother. He seemed very grown up and worldly, and I was impressed that he was in the British army. Paul was a very controlling person, and he wanted to manage every aspect of what I did. At the time I was exploring Tarot cards, and when Paul found out, he wouldn't let me have anything at all to do with them, and I had to throw them away. Paul and I got married when I was eighteen, and we lived for a while in Germany at an English army base. Together we had three children, two boys and a girl. Unsurprisingly, our marriage didn't last, and we separated about ten years later.

In my late twenties I had an overwhelming desire to start reading Tarot cards again. I hadn't touched any cards since Paul banned their use and made me get rid of mine. I bought myself a new pack, and when I started using them again, I kept getting pictures in my head of people who I instinctively knew were dead. I was somehow receiving information from these people, and the realisation came to me that maybe I was a medium. I needed to find answers for myself, and though I didn't know much at all about the Spiritualist religion, I thought that by attending a church service things would become clearer to me. No answers or help was forthcoming, and some long-term parishioners weren't very welcoming to me at all. I felt that this was a real shame because it went against everything I assumed would happen at the church.

Aged thirty-one I met a wonderful man called Nicholas, who everyone calls Nicky. We have been together for thirty-five years and married for seventeen of those. When I was with Paul, he hated me working and, like everything in my life, he had controlled that too. Nicky was happy that I wanted to get a job, and he supported my choice to do so. Nicky had his own business driving lorries. I started selling Tupperware at house parties, and immediately I was very successful at this. My boss recognised my selling abilities, and I soon became a manager with the company and I was given the role of training the other women in selling their products.

Once again I never seemed to feel truly happy in any of my jobs, even when I did well and I moved on from Tupperware. I continued selling goods at house parties, but this time it was racy underwear and 'naughty knickers'! A friend suggested I start my own business, so with only fifty pounds in working capital to buy my initial stock, away I went. I did really well with my party-plan sales, and I made enough money to buy Nicky a new lorry for his business.

One day when I was out I bought a copy of *Prediction*. It's not something I would normally read; I just felt compelled to buy it. When I opened the first page there was a photo of a place called the Arthur Findlay College, and it had my full attention. I had never heard of it, but I knew that I had to go there. I wasn't remotely sure what took place at any of the courses offered at the college, but it felt right, and I made a booking. I wasn't used to doing anything on my own. It wasn't something that I normally did, but this was different: I felt I had found what was always missing in my life.

Thankfully, Nicky was fine about me going. He had no interest at all personally, but he certainly wasn't controlling in any way, as I know many other spouses are when it comes to mediumship. We arrived together, and Nicky went upstairs with me to find my allocated bedroom. After he left I went down to dinner, and everyone at my table was talking about a man called Gordon, who would be performing a demonstration of mediumship that night, and everyone sounded very excited about it. My decision to attend the college was based purely on a 'knowing' that I was meant to be there and nothing more, so I had no idea who this 'Gordon' was.

We all squashed into the beautiful old library in readiness to watch Gordon Higginson, the college principal, perform his demonstration of mediumship. I was seated at the back of the room, and Gordon began the demonstration. I fully understood all of the evidence Gordon was bringing forward from the spirit communicator, but I was too nervous to put my hand up and say so. Gordon kept saying, 'Come on, I know you're in here.' Eventually, I put my hand up, and he proceeded to give me so much wonderful information from my loved one in spirit. Then he said, 'The spirit world has been waiting for you for a very long time, and now they have you you're going to be a very good medium. Now run along now and learn your craft.'

In that first year alone I went to the college for about twenty weeks in total. I was hooked on being there. I loved it, and I had finally found where I belonged in this world. Luckily, we lived nearby to the college, so I was able to attend as a day student, and I didn't stay over each night, like I did on my first visit. It was so much cheaper to come and go each day for the week, and it also meant that financially I could afford to attend more courses. Back then, in the late eighties and early nineties, you could stay overnight and complete a weekend course for a small cost, so I would do that too.

I met a wonderful friend called Jean Dallow at one of my many courses at Arthur Findlay, and we both went along to see a demonstration of physical mediumship being given by one of the tutors, Glyn Edwards. At this demonstration, Glyn came to me and said, 'You've got physical mediumship and you really should sit.' I didn't take any notice of what he said, as I was very happy working with my mediumship in the way I was. Glyn was an amazing medium and tutor, and sadly he is now in spirit himself.

Months later I went to another demonstration of physical mediumship, and the medium who was working came to me and said the same thing Glyn did. I mentally registered this, but again I did nothing else with it. I was staying at Jean's home, and we were doing what's called 'table tilting'; the moving table had me gently pinned up against the wall and wouldn't let me go. Jean tuned into what was happening with the table and why it wanted my attention so much. She said that I really needed to start listening to what I was being told, and I should start studying physical mediumship; that was the message she received from the spirit world via the table.

Table tilting is an age-old practice that mediums sometimes use to connect with the spirit world. Energy from two mediums is transferred through the table, by both gently resting their palms flatly upon it. If successful, and contact is made with the spirit world, the table will move about the room spelling out words using the alphabet by tapping on the participant's legs so many times, for each corresponding alphabetical letter. Demonstrations of this kind are done with the sitters being grouped in a large circle, and the table moves around in the middle of the ring. Meanwhile, the two mediums are still gently touching the tabletop with the palms of their hands. It's a wonderful phenomenon to witness, and we demonstrate it at the college at times.

I decided to buy a table to use for my own table tilting at home, so I bought a suitable sized one at a second-hand auction. My daughter, Kerry, is also a medium. At the time she was running a weekly development circle from the family home, and she thought it would be different and interesting to do table tilting one night with her students. I always sat in with the group at the circle, so this was fine by me, and I would help build the energy in the table with Kerry to get it moving initially.

Prior to us beginning the table tilting demonstration, Kerry had pre-warned her students that nothing at all might happen or there may be some spirit contact that would make the table move around in the circle. The students were all very excited and also extremely nervous, as none of them had seen it done before. Kerry and I put our hands gently on the table, and it felt immediately sticky and soft, and our fingers went through the actual wood. It was like touching melting butter, and it took my breath away. The table started to move around inside the circle, which frightened some of students, and I have to say that I was shocked by the intensity of it as well.

My interest in physical mediumship was immense, and Nicky kindly built me a special cabinet that is used for trance and physical mediumship demonstrations. The next week at circle, we decided to do an experiment to show the students what physical mediumship was like. This was very early days. Physical mediumship was quite new to me as well, and I had prepared the cabinet purely by using my own intuition about what was required. I lit a candle and placed it on a small table inside the cabinet and darkened everything so that whoever was sitting inside the cabinet could still be seen, but the room was in darkness.

The six students arrived, and when we entered the room where the cabinet sat, the energy was so intense. When I sat inside the cabinet and went into a trance state everyone present commented that I no longer had a physical face; everything was just white and I had no facial features at all. Then, one by one, other white faces with features began to appear over mine, both male and female of all ages. Each week more and more phenomena would happen, and there would be vortexes swirling around in the room and things would fly about. Kerry and I were fine with what was taking place; this is what physical mediumship is all about, but the circle members were all so frightened by what was happening that they stopped attending the circle, and it was disbanded, which was a shame.

When I was in my thirties I finally reconnected with my father and his side of the family again. I learnt very quickly that none of them approved of my mediumship, and because of my beliefs and abilities my father refused to speak to me again. My aunt wanted me to meet her side of the family, but I wasn't allowed to mention my mediumship because they wouldn't understand. Under these circumstances, I said that I wouldn't come at all. People wrongly assume that gypsies practise mediumship; they are very much into psychic readings but definitely not mediumship, in which we are communicating with the dead. Gypsies believe we should let the dead rest in peace, and we shouldn't connect with them.

About twenty-five years ago I was invited to start my teachers' training course at Arthur Findlay College, and to me this was such a wonderful honour to be asked. I teach at the college for about six weeks of the year, and I also do private one-on-one readings from home. I have been fortunate to travel overseas to teach students who I've met at the college. These students have invited me to run classes in their respective countries, and on these courses I do a mixture of private readings, workshops and platform demonstrations. I really enjoy the opportunity to work in this way, and to date I have taught in Hong Kong, the United States, Germany, The Netherlands, Spain and Iceland; it's all been amazing and I've loved it.

I go through stages with my mediumship, and I love working with all aspects of it. In the past it was all about physical mediumship, and I think I drove people mad with my obsession about it, but now it's very even, and I love doing all of the different modalities equally. The one thing I don't enjoy doing are spiritual assessments with the students at the college. These are personal verbal assessments about the person sitting before you, and all students have certain expectations about how they think they are progressing with their mediumship. Many are disappointed when they aren't told what they want to hear.

Everyone having the spiritual assessments hopes to be told that they are mediums, but many of the students just aren't there yet. I believe everyone has mediumship abilities within them, but some are better than others. It's like playing a piano; some can play a small tune with one finger and others can use a couple of fingers and possibly both hands at once. A handful will be naturally gifted and exceptional as mediums, and many will have scope, but they need years of dedicated practice to be any good.

I see some students who have nothing in the way of obvious mediumistic abilities, and they are incapable of achieving any form of spirit communication in the classroom, but I know I can help them in some other way. Students who are analytical cannot be mediums because they process everything that is happening, and therefore the naturalness of a spirit connection is impossible to be had. Mediums don't need to know the mechanics of mediumship; they just need to believe in it and it will happen for them. Analytical people are unable to have these same experiences.

Initially, I naively thought that healing was a very boring form of mediumship. Not long ago I received a phone call from the college to fill in for another tutor and to teach the healing course that week in their absence. I knew what to do, as I had completed many healing sessions as a student at the college over the years, but it wasn't ever something that interested me much. I went along, and I was immediately in love with performing and teaching this wonderful form of mediumship. I have since done further study to be accredited by the college, so I can now teach trance healing classes. Healers are all mediums, but they work in a different way: with healing the medium becomes a pure channel to the spirit world, but they are not to be receiving or making any contact with spirits; they are to simply allow the pure energy from the spirit world to pass through them directly to the person who is receiving healing.

My love of God is stronger now than ever. I've always felt his presence, and even though we weren't a religious family I feel that God and religion can be quite separate. You don't need to be religious to feel the presence of a greater power around you. I don't live a life that is restricted in any way by any religious dogma; my understanding of God is much simpler than that. God is a life force, a great energy who is there for whoever wants to believe in him, just as the spirit world is. It makes no sense to me at all that there are so many different religions worldwide that are so rich, and yet their worshippers are starving. That is not about God; that's about greed.

Years ago, when I first started doing my private sittings, I would ask for only a donation in payment, and most people would leave fifty pence. When the reading was over, if Nicky was home he would walk my clients out, and they would continually tell him how much they loved the reading and how they pay other mediums fifty pounds. After a while I started to charge a few pounds for a reading, but I was always very mindful about not charging too much money, because I knew that many of my clients couldn't afford to pay. You need to know when to give money back too, as sometimes the money you are receiving was meant to be used to put food on their table.

There have been so many amazing experiences relating to my readings, and one story in particular has always stayed with me because it was something that Nicky got to experience as well. I was doing a one-on-one sitting in our kitchen and unbeknown to me, Nicky had recently stored a dead car battery under the table, which he was going to try and recharge later on. As I was doing the reading the acid inside the battery started to bubble up and overflow onto the floor. I later showed Nicky, and he said it was impossible because it was a completely flat battery, yet it was somehow recharged because of the energy created from the reading.

Before I knew I was a medium, I had always been able to read random people, and I would use this natural ability to tap into the energy of complete strangers. I learnt very quickly not to do this because we shouldn't use our abilities to intrude into the private lives of others. I'm very mindful that mediumship isn't for everyone, but if I'm out and meet a stranger I will always be honest with them about what I do, but I will wait for them to ask me first. Being a medium is no different to being a hairdresser, accountant or bank teller, and you don't tend to announce your occupation as a way of opening any normal conversation.

My family is very supportive of what I do, and my mother was very proud of me being a medium; sadly, she passed in 2015. One of my grandchildren, Ben, is a medium. I was present at his birth, and I knew from the moment he was born that he had mediumship abilities. He is nineteen years old now, and we have never tried to dissuade him from what's happening, nor have we pushed him towards mediumship. What he does, or doesn't do, with his mediumship is his own choice. As a child, Ben spent a lot of time alone and away from the other children, which is often what happens with child mediums. Ben is also a wonderful natural healer, and even now at his young age he can heal people and animals through his touch.

Nicky and I got married at the college, and he was happy to marry in the Spiritualist Church, even though he is not of any religion himself. Nicky believes in what I do, which is very important to me, though he has only seen me demonstrate about three times at charity events. My grandchildren and Nicky recently overheard me doing some online Zoom readings with the students from the college, which I've been using because of the Covid-19 situation. They commented afterwards on how amazing it was and wanted to know, 'How did you do that?'

My mediumship has shown me many things, and because of it I'm not afraid to die at all. The hard part will be leaving my family behind, but I have no fear at all about what lays ahead.

Tutor and medium
Age, 66
Cheshunt in Hertfordshire, United Kingdom

sharon.harvey6@btinternet.com
www.sharonharveymedium.co.uk

Chapter seventeen

ANNE-MARIE BOND

In 2019 I met Anne-Marie at the college, where she was a last-minute fill-in as a guest trainee tutor for the week. I had a wonderful one-on-one mediumship sitting with Anne-Marie and, as always, Sam came through, giving all sorts of factual information and beautiful messages. Because I've had so many readings now with a mixture of my fellow students and tutors, Sam has become a brilliant communicator, and he always gives specific and clear information to whoever connects with him. Anne-Marie was spot-on, and I loved her friendly manner and the experience. Anne-Marie is London based and is a spiritual artist, coach and newly graduated tutor at Arthur Findlay College. She also works full-time as a design and delivery e-learning digital specialist.

Growing up, mediumship was certainly not something that was discussed in our home. I'm an only child, and I was christened in the Catholic church at St Margaret's in Lewisham, South London. My parents are not at all religious, so other than my christening, family church services did not play a part in my upbringing. My family heritage is Jamaican and Cuban; both of my parents are Jamaican born, and I have a great relationship with them.

Everyone has special childhood memories, and I'm no different. What is apparent to me now is how my awareness of the spirit world came about, but at the time it meant nothing at all to me. When I was young I had loads of Cindy dolls and other types as well, and I loved playing with them, but there was more to it for me. At nighttime I would put them all to bed in the cupboard and cover them up completely. My mother would ask me why I covered them, and I would tell her they came alive at night. There was also a life-sized doll I had to get rid of because I believed she too came alive at night, and as a six-year-old all of this really frightened me terribly. I understand now that it was the spirit world that I was seeing, but I blamed my innocent dolls.

Though my spiritual awareness was apparent as a child, at around fourteen years of age I developed a love for mystical things, and I discovered a real interest in Tarot cards. I was fascinated by books about the supernatural and life after death; I had an absolute fascination with things beyond the realms of this life. I began reading Tarot cards at home for myself and my friends. All of this was done in secret, and my parents weren't aware of my interest in the cards or anything else of this nature. Books helped me learn about many different aspects of metaphysical subjects. I began to read about psychic abilities and spiritual awareness, and this made me even more curious.

As I immersed myself in my Tarot cards I also dabbled in palm readings too. When I was seventeen I attended a party where I was asked to do a palm reading for my friend's boyfriend. As I started the reading people began to gather around, and I was so self-conscious because I didn't really know what I was doing. I was worried that everyone would think I was a fake. I knew I had some natural abilities, but the audience made me feel I couldn't do it. I read the guy's palm, and I said the first thing that came into my mind. I didn't have any concept of filtering what I saw, so I just blurted out, 'You're going to have an accident very soon, and you're almost going to die, but you will survive.' I would, of course, never say this to anyone now. Three weeks later in Deptford, London, this fellow was shot in the head at close range, and he nearly died but survived! I have never read a palm since because this reading was so accurate, and my own abilities frightened me.

I remember reading Tarot cards for a close female relative, and her husband was nearby listening to what I was saying. I said I could see another woman in the background, and I couldn't place her, but I knew that it wasn't my female relative. I said I don't know who she is, and I started joking and asking, 'Who is this woman?' Her husband had previously thought that the cards were rubbish, but he had suddenly gone very quiet. A couple of weeks later my relative found out that he was having an affair and that was the other woman who I saw in the cards.

It was obvious that I was very capable at reading Tarot cards, so at aged nineteen I turned professional, and I went around the country getting paid to read my cards at psychic fairs. I established a wonderful reputation for accuracy, and I had a huge following of repeat clientele. I was also very young-minded for a nineteen-year-old and quite naive, so when I was invited by an Italian man called Marcus to join his development circle I immediately agreed to, though I didn't know what a circle was. At the circle I had no idea what was going on, and Marcus hadn't explained anything either, but I stayed for six months.

At that stage in my life I still didn't know what mediumship was, and I continued doing psychic readings using my Tarot cards. I had a friend who was a devout Christian, and he was like a brother to me. My friend believed that my card readings were conjuring up evil spirits, and it was wrong to do so. I explained to him it wasn't evil or wrong, and I was attempting to help people through my readings. Regardless, my friend's warning made me wonder if reading the cards was indeed wrong, so I decided it wasn't what I wanted to do anymore, and I gave up reading Tarot cards for the next fifteen years. My large collection of different Tarot decks were all thrown away, and this was like a bereavement for me, as some of those cards were quite old and some were very rare.

In my mid-thirties I was a self-employed contractor conducting information technology training with a variety of companies. I managed to save the company that I was contracted to half a million pounds in needless expenditure. Regardless of this great result, my boss said he wasn't sure if they had the funding to extend my working contract. I had also been promised a monetary bonus based on my results, and I intuitively knew that something didn't feel right; my bonus and contract extension were never forthcoming.

Feeling very disillusioned, I wondered if reading Tarot cards would work for me again, just as they had done in the past. It had been fifteen years since I last read Tarot, so it was time to buy myself a new pack and to go to work. I thought I would need some Tarot training because it had been so long. I looked online and found an advertisement for a woman called Marie Claire, who offered lessons. I called Marie to enquire about the Tarot classes, and she said it would take me many weeks to learn everything. I don't know why I didn't just trust that everything would come back to me, as I finished all that we were to learn in the first session. Regardless, I kept going to the classes because I liked Marie and she taught me how to use many different card spreads.

There was another woman in my class, called Tracey. She and I would take it in turns to read the cards for one another, and we soon became the best of friends. Tracey could feel the presence of spirits in a room, and when this happened her ears would go red. When she first told me this I made her stop talking because I wanted nothing at all to do with any conversation about spirits.

With my rediscovered confidence in reading Tarot cards I found online a woman called Michele Knight, who was running a well-known psychic phone line business, and I rang the number. Michele was known as the X-Factor resident celebrity psychic. I was told that someone from the company would call me to give a test reading to see if I was any good or not. To my amazement, Michele rang me herself, and I was assessed on the Tarot reading I did for her over the phone. Fortunately, Michele was impressed by what I told her, and she offered me a job to do Tarot card readings with her company. I started to feel happier in myself and in my new-found confidence that was very much present when I did my psychic phone readings. I had learnt to speed read, which was a requirement of the company, and I really enjoyed my work and helping the callers.

Months later I was going to see my hairdresser, Dionne, and as I was driving to the salon it felt like there was another energy in the car. I still had no idea about mediumship, and the spirit world unnerved me. I wasn't sure what to do, so I said 'hello' and a voice answered 'hello' back. Still having no idea what was happening I said, 'What's your name?' To be honest I was being a bit cocky, and then I heard the name 'Marcus'. Feeling shocked, I said, 'Tell me something that's going to happen today that I couldn't possibly know about.' I then heard, 'Your hairdresser has left.' I thought this was all rubbish, as I had my confirmed appointment with Dionne. I didn't believe anything that was happening, but I still couldn't explain what I had just experienced. After arriving at the hairdresser's I was told by Flo, the owner of the salon, that Dionne had left the business very suddenly. The shock was too great for me; my mind was everywhere, and I couldn't sign on to do my shift on the psychic phone lines later on that day.

The next day, just before going online to do my Tarot readings, I once again felt an unseen presence in the room. I said out loud, 'Okay, if this is real and you want me on board, tell me something about my callers today.' I heard the names, 'Cathy, Arthur and bluebells', and I knew the information given related to my second caller of the day. Before I started to do the phone reading for the second caller, I asked this random client if she knew the name Cathy, relating to someone who was in spirit. The woman said that Cathy was her mother's good friend and that she passed away some time ago. I then asked her if the name Arthur meant anything at all to her. My caller said that Arthur was the name of a newborn baby in the family. I was holding my head by this stage, and I was trying to rationalise everything. I then asked if bluebells meant anything at all to her, and she said Cathy had been a great gardener who loved bluebells, and she had planted bluebells in her own garden to remind her of Cathy. The spirit world now had my full attention.

Through my friend Tracey, I joined a spiritual development circle in Lewisham, London. The woman running the group introduced us to some psychic exercises, and as the weeks progressed she started talking about mediumship and she gave a plausible explanation of what it was. After that I started to enjoy the classes, and I wasn't so afraid of exploring mediumship or the spirit world. Oddly, I then started to recall that many years beforehand I had attended another circle group run by the Italian man, Marcus, but I had somehow swept all of those memories from my mind.

In my late thirties I realised there were Spiritualist churches in the United Kingdom; until then I had never heard of them or even noticed any. The first Spiritualist church I ever entered was on Well Hall Road in Eltham, and on that occasion I took my cousin along with me. We sat quietly at the back. Neither of us had any idea about what was going to take place. There were hymns being sung, music was being played and an open address was given by the minister. Later on in the service a mother and daughter called June and Peggy were introduced, and they were the two mediums. I was impressed by June, the mother, and even though I didn't understand anything about mediumship, I thought she was good because everything she was saying seemed to make sense to whoever she was reading for.

Then it was Peggy's turn. She stood up and talked about a big rabbit that she could see hopping down the aisle, and I innocently started looking for an actual rabbit. No-one else seemed to be searching for the animal, and my brain told me it was all make-believe, and this performance really turned me right off. To me it was fake, and I abandoned my spiritual search yet again. This time it was for another three months.

My curiosity got the better of me: I went back to my circle group and I returned to the same church in Eltham. This time the platform demonstration I experienced was truly amazing, and it got me hooked.

After that I started to allow myself to awaken at last with my own mediumship unfoldment. It was at the Light on the Hill Spiritual Church in Dartford that I saw the highly respected medium Tony Stockwell for the first time in person. I had seen him on YouTube only. He was a wonderful medium, and I wondered if he would be the same in person. I was amazed by Tony's demonstration, and after that day Tony made me a true believer in mediumship and how it helps to heal all those who receive a spirit communication. I intuitively knew which car Tony drove, and afterwards I went out to the car park, and I wrote him a brief note of gratitude: 'Thank you for restoring my belief that this is real by the evidence that I have seen today.' I left it on his windscreen.

I finally understood that my own mediumistic journey was going to be so different from there on. I started to meditate at home for the first time, and it came very easily to me. The Spiritualist church in Eltham ran an open platform night, and I decided to go along and see what it was all about. On these nights anyone can stand up on the platform and try to make a connection with the spirit world. Before I went I said to spirit that I needed to finally develop my mediumship, and I also needed to find someone to help me do this.

As I entered the church a woman who was unknown to me was standing there, and she invited me to join a private closed circle in Bexley that she ran. The same woman then invited me to do a demonstration that night, and before I knew it I had said, 'Yes please!' The words just came out. I had not initially intended to do anything; I was there only to observe and learn. I walked up to the platform and turned, then I saw the audience and panicked. I had no real training, and I still didn't understand much about mediumship.

I somehow managed to do the demonstration, and it was successful. I then started attending the private circle in Bexley for twelve months. My abilities started to show, and my teacher took me and two other students with her to do demonstrations at various Spiritualist churches. At these services I would hear people in the congregation say, 'She's going to be really good.' I had no belief or confidence in what I did, but everyone was whispering about me, and my readings were repeatedly successful. I was thankful to always be allowed to work with Maureen Ridgewell, who was the most advanced in our group alongside another medium called Alison.

Soon I was doing four or five platform demonstrations a week at different churches. Previously, I was fascinated to watch these brave mediums who would stand at the front of the church communicating with spirit, and now I was one of them. Before this I had always been very reclusive, but my mediumship got me out of the house and helped with me deal with my feelings of depression. Quite quickly I developed a thirst to learn more, and I began to fully immerse myself in any way I could.

To develop my mediumship properly I started on the educational route, firstly with the Spiritualist National Union and then two courses back-to-back at Arthur Findlay College. My old friend Tracey had told me about the college, though she had never been there herself. In 2010 I completed my first weekend and week-long courses at the college. The weekend course was with a lovely Dutch medium called José Gosschalk, and on the following week, my two tutors were Stella Upton and Simone Key. José Gosschalk was the first medium to give me a real understanding of the type of medium I wanted to become. It was José's gentle nature that prevented me from having a flight moment. I felt totally at home over that weekend with her and very much included in all we did in José's classes.

The next week at the college was a very different experience. I didn't feel as included as I had on the weekend, but I still felt safe in the hands of my tutor, Stella, who was very supportive to the needs of everyone in her class. I left the college knowing there was something special within me, but because of my lack of confidence it still took me another two years to go any further with my studies and to believe that I was a medium.

After my two-year break I started attending many courses at the college, intentionally booking with lots of different tutors. I believe training with many tutors is a great way to learn, as they all have something special and unique to offer the students. I have been to the college countless times now, and one year I went eleven times on a combination of weekend and week-long courses.

At one of my many courses, Simone Key told me I needed to start running my own weekly development circle. If you know Simone, she doesn't say that to everybody. Simone knew nothing about my background, yet she felt I had much to offer as a teacher. In my typical style it took me two weeks to decide, and even then I had to ask the spirit world to help me make the right decision. Simone was right: I started the circle, and I enjoyed sharing my knowledge very much with my students. I'm especially grateful to Owen French, who was one of my students initially. Owen later ran the circle in my absence for over a year. Owen is a wonderful healer, Tarot reader, spiritual counsellor and friend, who gives his time freely to those seeking guidance.

My parents now know what I do as a medium, but for many years they didn't have any idea at all. I would describe my mother as very conservative, and she is not into any of what I do. I know that Mum is naturally very psychic, so therefore anything to do with psychic abilities and mediumship really frightens her, just as I reacted initially. It felt very much like I was 'coming out of the closet' when I told my parents about my mediumship, but I wanted them to be aware of what I was doing. One of my mother's friends used to come to me for Tarot readings, which was great, because it normalised what I did to my mother. Another of Mum's friends doesn't approve of what I do, and she believes that I've gone to the devil's side.

As a part of my initial mediumship training, I joined another circle for a year run by Lynn Probert, a very gifted medium and tutor at the college. Lynn was running the circle from Tony Stockwell's centre in Wickford, Essex, where I have attended many wonderful workshops run by Tony. At the time, my father thought I might have been involved in a cult of some kind, so to stop him thinking this I decided to take my parents to Arthur Findlay College to see Tony do a mediumship demonstration at a special event being held there. They agreed to attend, and afterwards I introduced my parents to Tony. My father said later that he wasn't converted in his beliefs, but he felt more agreeable and comfortable about me spending so much time in my development circles and at the college.

In 2014 I won the Gordon Higginson Scholarship at the Barbanell Conference Centre in Stafford. I felt like a real medium after this. Initially, I wasn't going to enter, and I cried for fifteen minutes when I received the letter saying I had won. It is a very prestigious award, with the wonderful prize of three complementary weeks of training at the Barbanell Centre spread over three years and three weekends, with an assigned a mentor.

My mentor was Colin Bates, a wonderful medium, tutor and now friend. Colin was instrumental in helping me, and I know he had my back and constantly supported me during that time. In June and

August 2019, I was asked to assist both Simone Key and Chris Drew on their respective weeks at Arthur Findlay, and I worked as one of the trainee tutors, teaching my own groups for the entire week. I also gave tutorials and lectures to the college students and provided private readings and spiritual assessments as well. In early 2021, I completed my tutor training studies at Arthur Findlay College and am now what's called a Tutor of Tomorrow.

Seven years ago, spirit art just came to me, and I had a real need to draw something. I can't draw at all normally, but I was being gently driven by spirit to draw the images they wanted me to see. Some of my drawings have been done in the dark or by using a red light, as many of them are done in the middle of the night or whenever spirit wakes me and pushes me to draw. Spirit art is a visual representation of what the spirit communicator looked like physically in appearance at some point in their lifetime.

Spirit seems to understand the drawing ability of the medium, and they show themselves in that representation, so the medium artist can best capture their appearance in the artwork. They may look as they did when they passed or at an earlier stage in their life – whatever captures them in the best light and will be recognisable to their loved ones. One of my drawings was of a woman in spirit who looked very familiar to me, and it turned out to be my own grandmother. I had a photograph of her in the other room. I went and got it, and the likeness was amazing. This was spirit's way of giving me confirmation that I was tapping into the spirit world with my artwork.

At one of the courses I was attending at the college, I met a fellow student called Robbie. Robbie asked me to do a spirit drawing for him, and I agreed. Initially, I tried drawing the spirit person's face, and for some reason I couldn't. Then I started drawing in just browns and yellows, which is not my normal colour palette. As I continued to connect with the spirit communicator, I said to Robbie, 'This woman unfortunately died in a fire,' and I also shared the additional information that I had received. Robbie told me it was his mother, and she had tragically died that way. Robbie was very moved by the whole experience, and he gifted me a book about spirit art that he bought especially from the college bookshop.

A while ago the spirit world started to tell me to work in oils. I had never used that type of paint before, and I wasn't totally sure if I could paint successfully in that way. Finally, I was getting much better at listening to spirit and their suggestions, so I went out and bought a brand called Van Gogh oil paints. I did a couple of paintings, and the new paints worked so well for me; I was amazed by the results. No matter how good my spirit art is I still struggle in calling myself an artist, as I still can't draw unless I'm working under the guidance of the spirit world.

I currently teach mediumship online to my students, and I also teach spirit art and demonstrate spirit portrait art. Spirit portrait art can be done alone, and it can also be achieved when working with another medium. The other medium makes a connection with a spirit communicator and gives verbal evidence of their survival. Meanwhile, I link in with the same spirit communicator, and my role is to create a likeness to the spirit person's living physical image from what I can 'see'. The recipient who is present then verifies if the evidence being given is accurate or not and acknowledges if there is also a true likeness in the image I have drawn. It is quite fascinating to see this done.

In addition to my art I also conduct private readings, and I mentor in one-on-one coaching on various subjects online. I'm also writing my own book, called Life is Short, which is a journal format designed to help people put their life in order and to live life before transitioning from this world. I still work full-time as a design and delivery e-learning specialist (digital), where I design and deliver e-learning interactive training videos in the IT field. I also create animation videos for small spiritual businesses to help promote them online. At work most of my colleagues know about my mediumship and my spirit art, and this makes life a lot easier to explain.

Money can often be a sore point when it comes to mediumship. I believe that mediums should charge for their readings and for any tuition they offer. All well-trained mediums invest a huge amount of money in their own training and advancement in their learning. There is simply no reason why mediums shouldn't charge for their work, and I've never understood the argument that we should all work for nothing, in thanks for our God-given abilities.

I'm not afraid to die at all. Before discovering my mediumship abilities there were many times I would have been happy for God to call me home, but since then I'm now really enjoying life, and I realise I have so much to live for. I'm more worried about my parents if I were to die, as I'm their only child. I'm also strangely concerned about the logistics of someone else having to tidy and pack up my home once I die. But death itself is not frightening, providing I die in my own bed in my sleep!

I run monthly online masterclasses in a wide array of subjects, and I see my creativity as having the capacity to span over more than just one topic. Hearing a person who can speak another language fluently is wonderful, and I see my creativity in the same way. I used to play the piano, and we still have one in the family home. I also used to dance on stage in my younger years. Creativity is within me and a big part of who I am. I guess I have always been involved working with the public in some way, and mediumship is the most incredible way to be of service to both the spirit world and the world where we live.

Spiritualist medium, spiritual artist, coach and tutor
Age, 50
Design and delivery e-learning digital specialist
London, United Kingdom

www.theportraitofspirit.com
spiritualstars@gmail.com

Chapter eighteen

Debra Chalmers

Debra was at Arthur Findlay College on my first visit in early 2015, and we sat at the same dining table for all of our meals that week. I knew from speaking with Debra that she was much more experienced with her mediumship than I was; it was all just beginning for me and it sounded like Debra knew what she was doing. I have since bumped into Debra a few times over the years on other courses at the college. Debra's warm and engaging manner, together with her previous career as a nurse, made me very curious to learn how her mediumship unfolded. Debra lives in the United Kingdom, works full-time as a practising medium and teaches mediumship.

I come from a very open family in which we speak about most things, and nothing is ever really out of bounds. I had a great aunt who read tea leaves, and apparently all sorts of strange things happened around her. It was all regarded as quite normal, and no-one minded her unusual ways. My biological father, Bob, was known to be a medium, and even though I had no contact with him I did find this to be very interesting. My stepdad, George, was very mediumistic as well; mediums tend to run in my family, and in those families it is regarded as completely acceptable. I should point out that the family wouldn't use the terms 'medium' or 'mediumship'; it would more likely be described as 'experiencing the presence of ghosts'.

My great-grandmother, Hannah, was mediumistic, but she wouldn't have called herself that either. Hannah could hear spirits, and she once heard a voice saying, 'Hannah, Hannah, you're rich.' And after learning this, we all wondered if she might be going to win the lottery! We later realised that it was a lovely message from spirit telling her how lucky she was. Hannah had everything in life she needed: she had a good family, brilliant health (even in her nineties) and she had the right approach to life, which meant she truly had a wonderful life, and all of this made her 'rich'. The importance of that wonderful spirit message was never lost on her, or on me either.

My childhood began in the city of Durham in County Durham, in North East England. I was born and bred there, and it's where I live today with my husband, Fraser, and our two daughters, Charlotte and Katie, were born there too. My stepdad, George, raised me, and I've always regarded him as my father. George came into my life when I was four years old, and he and my mother, Beverley, married when I was six. Mum and George had a wonderful marriage, and our home life was always very stable and happy for my brother, Dean, and me.

When we were older Mum went back to university and completed a degree in social work, and then she got her master's. She worked so hard to achieve this; it was an incredible effort that made us all so proud. My mother is now a qualified social worker based in the hospital system, where she primarily works with older people. Sadly, George passed away in 2014 from lung cancer. George was also a very hard worker, and he was employed by private companies and sometimes the council, laying roads all over the surrounding areas of our county.

My family was not very religious, and there was no pressure for me to follow any religion. The choice was mine to make, and I very much enjoyed having an upbringing that was not a strict one. When I was about ten I attended a Methodist Sunday school, but this was something I chose to do for myself, and my mother arranged it. To be honest I didn't really enjoy the classes at all, but I liked the woman who ran them, so I kept on going.

Mum and I were curious about the local Spiritualist church in the nearby town of Spennymoor, which was commonly known as the 'spooky place'. We both decided to attend together. The church was cosy and warm, and I was the youngest person there by at least thirty years. I was only sixteen at the time, but I felt I truly belonged, and it was a unique feeling. Neither of us knew what happened there; we just started attending, and then we realised that mediums were a part of the weekly service.

My mother had it in her head that if we kept going to the church for over a year, we would be invited to join a 'secret circle', but of course this never ever happened. Somehow, Mum made this strange assumption and was disappointed when no-one asked us to join this non-existent covert group. Mum always hoped she had mediumship abilities herself, and she loved watching the mediums work. Each week after the service, she would say to me, 'Let's go mingle with the mediums.' She enjoyed being around them, and as we had our cup of tea afterwards she always hoped to receive a little personal message from them. From the very first time we attended, the mediums would come up to us and say to my mother, 'She's got it; she can do it,' and I didn't know what they were talking about. I now know they recognised my untapped mediumship abilities.

My awareness of spirit started at a very young age, and then it quickly diminished, only to return again in my teenage years and then, nothing again. Strangely, my connection to the spirit world would just come and go without notice, and as it reappeared I would say to myself, 'I forgot I could do that.' When I did finally embrace my ability to sense the spirit world and communicate with them, it stayed with me. It took me a long time to fully acknowledge my own mediumship abilities, because from what little I knew of other mediums I seemed to do things quite differently to them. I could sense a presence when I was giving my messages, but because it wasn't a clear vision, I assumed I wasn't working as a 'real medium' would.

When I was young I had many experiences with the spirit world, and I presumed when the real mediums were working on the platform in church they would have much stronger and more realistic experiences compared to what I had received as a little girl. I didn't understand that mediumship is subjective, so when the mediums were describing the physical description of the woman in spirit standing behind me, I would be searching and asking, 'Where? I can't see her.' Because I couldn't see her with my physical eyes, I didn't acknowledge that I could be a medium because I didn't understand the mechanics of how mediumship worked.

In 1996, when I was twenty years old, I started my training as a nurse, and by that stage it felt so long since I had experienced the spirit world around me. At the same time I started to become more aware of my psychic abilities, and I would intuitively know how the people around me were feeling and what was going on in their lives. All of this triggered my mediumistic abilities, and I began to have contact with the spirit world once again.

As a student nurse I worked at the Durham County Hospital, and once I was fully qualified I was offered a full-time post to work there, so I decided to stay on. I was working with very sick patients in the oncology and haematology ward of the hospital. The patients were of all age groups, the young and the old and everything in between. My mediumship wasn't happening all the time. I was so busy with my work, and I had no idea or pre-warning when I was going to experience the presence of the spirit world around the patients.

The hospital was very old fashioned, and it had old and outdated 'Nightingale' wards, with all of the beds in one big room, divided in two long rows along opposite walls. I had just qualified as a nurse and was working the nightshift. Part of the nightly routine was to go around and close the curtains surrounding each patient's bed, to give them some degree of privacy as they slept. As another nurse and I sat at the bottom of the ward the curtains were blowing and moving seemingly by themselves. It wasn't dramatic, but we could both see it happening. My colleague said, 'Can you see that curtain moving?' I said yes, but what I could also see was a spirit woman standing there moving them about! It wasn't at all scary; the woman just wanted to be around her loved one, and she was letting her presence be known to me.

On another night in my ward everyone had been given their nightly medications and were fast asleep. I sat at my desk finalising my paperwork under the light of a small desk lamp. Instantly I felt a male in spirit in the room, and I knew it was a patient's husband. I saw him, and he motioned for me to go and check on his wife. He was pointing to a bed and he said, 'I've taken her.' This particular female patient had been well a short time earlier, and her death wasn't at all expected. When I looked in on my patient she had indeed passed, but she looked so happy and at total peace. Her husband was there to be with her as she passed from this life to the next. It was a beautiful and memorable experience for me to witness.

In a particular ward there were patients who were terribly sick, and whenever I was with them I got a real sense that their families in spirit were nearby, ready and waiting to help them cross to the spirit world. Many of the other nurses experienced these feelings as well, and we would often comment to one another, 'Did you feel that?' or 'Did you see that?' These nurses also had a knowing about the impending deaths of these patients, and we all called it nurses' intuition.

In 2007 I began to do private mediumship sittings after work, and eventually it became really hard for me time-wise to work full-time, look after my family and do readings two or three nights a week. I didn't have the discipline or knowledge to stick to any time frames, and my readings would go for thirty minutes or up to an hour and a half. It was all getting out of hand, and it wasn't practical or feasible to be trying to do all that I was.

There was a great demand for my readings. All of my clients came from referrals, and I knew many of them wouldn't ever attend a Spiritualist church to receive a spirit communication but were comfortable in coming to me. I was very aware that what I offered helped so many grieving people to heal in some way, simply by being reconnected with their loved ones during a reading.

It was a very difficult decision, but I knew that something had to give: I had to choose between my nursing career or my love of doing my mediumship readings. Because I hadn't had any formal teaching with my mediumship, I felt I should continue doing what I was professionally trained to do, and that was working in the health sector. I tried to pull back and stop doing my readings, and every time I attempted this someone would beg me for a sitting to help them with their grief, so I was constantly being pulled back into it.

I had made my choice, but the spirit world clearly had other ideas. At the time I was working in senior management and running the sexual health services across County Durham and North Yorkshire. It was a very busy time; we were in the process of restructuring the whole department, and suddenly I had the realisation that I didn't want to do this type of high-pressure work anymore. I felt an overwhelming calling to leave the National Health Service and work full-time as a medium.

My mind was made up, and as the manager, I was able to give the department a workable plan, without the need to replace me in my well-paid position. They accepted my proposal, and the redundancy package they gave me created a much-needed cushion to pay bills and expenses until my full-time mediumship business took off. By this stage I had been a healthcare professional for thirteen years.

In 2011 my mediumship business began in full swing. I finally started to charge clients for their readings, and I became very busy immediately. I had decided on no more home visits; everyone came to our home, and I worked from a designated space there. This was a much more workable solution, and it fit in well with Fraser and the girls. They were all very aware of my role as a medium, and no-one even talked about it. It was just what Mum does.

A couple of years later I saw an advertisement for the Arthur Findlay College, and I was really drawn to the ad and wondered what went on there. I decided I had to attend, so I chose a course that fitted in well with a gap in my existing bookings. I had no idea about any of the tutors conducting the classes – their names meant nothing at all to me – but I felt that the spirit world was guiding me towards finding the right course that suited my needs.

I was very nervous. We always travelled together as a family, and this was my first trip away alone. At the college I met and made new friends straight away, and there was nothing to be frightened of at all. We were all so like-minded, and many were first-timers just like me. This wonderful experience allowed me to understand how important it was to receive proper tuition in how I worked as a medium. Once I started my formal training, my mediumship improved greatly because I learnt how to deal with my own blockages, those self-created barriers that I had inadvertently been putting in front of myself.

Prior to going to the college I sometimes felt very alone with what I was doing in my work, as there was no-one I could properly share my problems and questions with. My tuition taught me many things, including the importance of meditating on a regular basis and how being in a natural altered state of mind allowed me to become more in tune with myself. This improved my mediumship. I've now attended nearly twenty weeks of courses at the college, and the students and tutors have become like a special type of family to me.

After my initial training at Arthur Findlay I branched out and did further mediumship study at the Zwanenhof Spiritual Centre in The Netherlands, where I've been on a few occasions and really enjoyed it. I have also completed numerous weekly and weekend courses at the Barbanell Centre in Stafford in the United Kingdom, which I love. The financial and personal investment I've made in myself has been very beneficial, not just for me but for my clients too, and most importantly to the spirit world, which we ultimately serve.

My mediumship work has allowed me to travel overseas doing a mixture of demonstrations, teaching and holding private sittings in Spain, Germany and The Netherlands. Each experience has been very special and life changing in its own way, and I'm so grateful for these wonderful opportunities to work in this way. The church services I attend as the medium are all voluntary, and I love demonstrating this way, as there's usually a wonderful atmosphere. The congregation are open and accepting of mediumship, and it's often what brings them along to the services in the first place.

With my work I go through all types of phases in which I might concentrate more on platform demonstrations or teaching than one-on-one sittings, or at other times I may focus on soul work. I really like to vary things a lot, and I love going through these different stages, where I feel that the spirit world is directing which facet I will concentrate on. In 2019 I did a lot of one-on-one sittings. That phase is just ending now, and my focus recently has moved back to teaching mediumship. I love the changes as I always feel it keeps me fresh in my work.

It doesn't really surprise me that a lot of nurses come to me for mediumship training, and I've met many students at Arthur Findlay who are nurses as well. It's neither uncommon or unexpected, as nurses are constantly dealing with death, and therefore the spirit world, as part of their daily work. Universally, nurses are people who care for humanity, and they want to be of service to others, so it's not unusual to see them exploring mediumship at all. They are also often very sensitive people, and you must have a high level of sensitivity to be able to connect with those in spirit.

My mediumship has caused stress for me personally. When I first started working full-time as a medium I put a lot of undue pressure on myself on many levels. I would always be worried if I was good enough in the reading and if I was I able to make my clients feel more at peace afterwards. Looking back I was very hard on myself, and it wasn't warranted at all. From the very beginning I worked hard in setting up my business properly and in seeking proper tuition for myself and my mediumship. I felt this personal pressure to bring the world and more to my clients at every reading, but all I really needed to do was to get out of the way of myself and just allow the spirit communication to take place naturally.

The two closest people I've lost to the spirit world are my stepdad, George, and my great-nan, Hannah (my grandmother's mother), who we lived with for a while when we were young. I communicate with them both, and I love doing this. Before my great-nan died I had a dream about her, in which her own mother was there. I recognised my great-nan's mother because I knew her when I was a teenager. Her mother said to me, 'You know that we're taking her, don't you?' In this extremely vivid dream there was also my own mother, and we were both told to say our goodbyes and to get ready, because they would be coming back for her.

A few months later my great-nan passed away, and I feel I was being given the opportunity to take more time to be with her and to enjoy the newly made memories of being together during those last few months. The spirit world won't normally tell you in advance when a loved one is dying – no-one is to know that – but this was more like a gentle prompt to spend this quality time with my great-nan.

My great-nan came back in spirit within twenty-four hours of her passing, and she was so clear and strong in what she told me. My mother is a bit of a drama queen, and because of this my great-nan was mad with her, and she said to me, 'Tell her what did she want me to do, wait till I was one hundred? Because she's spoiling my party!' I told my mother what my great-nan had said about living to be one hundred. and my mum replied, 'Debra, I have a photo of her here, and I just said to her, 'Why couldn't you live till you were one hundred!' My great-nan was obviously aware of what my mother had said, and that's why she came through to me with this funny and wonderful message.

Mediumship is often totally misunderstood because we live in a very black and white objective world that is evidence and science based. We want to be able to touch it so then maybe we will believe in it, but mediumship doesn't work like that; it's not tangible, it's subjective. Because of this it frightens many people, and unfortunately there will always be fraudulent psychics and mediums, and these people give everyone a bad name and the whole sector a shoddy reputation.

In the beginning I was constantly having to justify what I do as a medium, as everyone seemed to have an opinion about it, which was often, 'I don't know if I believe in that.' What I find odd is that no-one would ever say that about any other job, but sadly they do in relation to mediumship. It's no different to saying 'I'm a plumber' and someone replies, 'Oh, I don't know if I believe in plumbers!' Maybe it's just that mediumship conjures up the fear of the unknown; it's shrouded in mystery, and people are wrongly fearful of looking at it for what it is: a simple communication between a living person and a person in spirit.

Over the years a few friends have drifted apart since I've become so involved in my work as a medium. There hasn't been a real falling out in any way; it's more of a moving away from one another. As this has happened new people have come into my life, and many of them are like-minded. I have some old friends who are quite spiritual themselves. There are others who don't approve of my work, and they simply can't accept or understand that I am a medium. One old friend, who is a complete atheist, thought I was being quite fanciful and deceitful of those who came to me for a reading, and this really upset me. How could a so-called friend think I was being duplicitous to other people? I didn't feel I had to justify to her what I do as a medium. I was not asking her to justify her non-belief in anything. We gave each other a wide berth after that.

As a person I feel I have matured a lot through my mediumship. I'm still the same old Debra, but a part of me has personally grown. I am now calmer as a person, and I'm less anxious than I was before. I don't struggle as I would have earlier. I'm in my own bubble, and I can deal with things so much better now. That's very empowering. Mediumship brings about a real positiveness in knowing that everything in life will work out the way it's meant to.

Medium and former nurse
Age, 45
Durham, United Kingdom

debra.chalmers@rocketmail.com
www.debrachalmers.com

Chapter nineteen

Andres Engracia

Andres is the youngest contributor here, and we first met in 2017 after I sent my manuscript to the publishing company in Sydney where he worked. I found Andres to always be fun, personable and warm, and he assisted me in having my first book published. It was also very apparent to me that Andres had mediumship abilities of his own, which he later confirmed. Andres and I have since formed a lovely friendship, and I was very interested in learning more about this fascinating young man. Originally from the Philippines and raised in Australia, Andres is currently living in Sydney. Andres has created and published a number of Oracle card sets that are sold internationally and locally.

When I was around eight years old, a neighbour of ours died suddenly, and even at this really young age I began to consider and contemplate the concept of death and dying. It was also at this early stage in my life that I saw a spirit manifest from its ethereal form into a human figure before my eyes. I have never seen a spirit appear in the same fashion since, and it was then I realised that the supernatural world was real.

I later came across books on the subject. Every psychic or medium described was always female, and so I ascertained that intuitive skills were granted only to the feminine; I didn't know that men could 'receive' these gifts as well, and so I didn't seek out a path to 'grow into' my own untapped abilities.

My mother raised me to be a good Catholic boy – attending church on Sundays, weekend prayer nights and holding altar rituals for saints and spirits. I kept my routines but discarded the rest as I grew older. I formed my own ties of spirituality, shifting and changing through my own personal experiences as they came and went. My mother definitely had vast intuitive abilities herself, and when I mentioned my own psychic perceptions, they were always met with a nonchalant reception. Her reaction was not too dissimilar to many Hispanic/European cultures of families, which funnelled all supernatural existence directly into Christian-based spirituality.

I was born in the Philippines. My mother was Filipino, and my father is Irish, from Scottish descent, and I have never met him. Although I was raised along Australia's east coast by my mom and a stepfather during my childhood, I never felt completely at home in Australia and hungered to live abroad, being drawn to Scotland and Ireland, before Mom ever mentioned details about my biological father.

Growing up as an only child and an immigrant boy surrounded by mostly Australian families, I spent a lot of my time alone, and I was happy to be left to my own thoughts in assimilating to my new surroundings, the language and new worldview. I immersed myself in books about old magick and supernatural occurrences, and I took these publications to the outback bushes around my home, where I could read them away from prying and judgemental adult eyes. Looking back at those times and thinking of the decisions I made so strongly for myself, it's simple to say that my curiosity about spiritual texts and experiences were both an escaping comfort and a happy interest, not too different from a child who finds passion in dancing or drawing. A potential interest for things to come.

I was extremely close to my mother, and my whole world was tipped upside down in 2001 when she died from cervical cancer at only forty-one years of age. I was ten at the time, about to turn eleven. As an only child, I wasn't given a choice, and I didn't have a voice to express what I wanted, so I stayed with my stepfather for the next year. I knew I didn't want to continue living with him, so I made my own plans to stay with another family. Initially, I moved in with my best mate from school and his family, and I lived there for about two years, from the age of twelve to fourteen. Unfortunately, another tragedy struck in my life when my childhood friend, Danny, passed in a horrific car accident. It was another incredibly challenging time in my life, and I was only just starting to slowly come to terms with life without my mom, and now Danny. The situation became too much for me to bear, and my rebellious self decided to spin fortune's wheel once more.

Losing my mother and my friend culminated in a tremendous turning point for me, in recognising how very little people knew about managing death and trauma themselves, let alone guiding a young teenager to understand and manage it. We all figure out these things on our own. I definitely made terrible decisions and choices over the years, and while I still don't have it all right, I don't regret the lessons I gained by learning from those mistakes made. I didn't have the normal family life that I craved, but that didn't mean I couldn't learn to be the guardian and family for my own heart's sake. At sixteen years of age, I began living on my own as an independent, and that situation stamped me with a unique reputation among my schoolmates. While I mostly took it for granted at the time, it did enable me certain experiences, in which I had to forcefully mature myself ahead of the others in so many ways.

I also had to admit to myself a number of times that I had no-one else to blame for my mistakes, and as unsteady as my naive behaviour often was, these reality checks did give me courage to take ownership of my choices, while navigating life as a growing adult. I worked on my creativity, I read the books that I always wanted to read, I watched supernatural horror films in the early mornings before school, and boy, did I cry myself to sleep almost every night. Mistakes and tragedies make us human and for me, those experiences as an independently living teenager were my first sail-flag in steering myself towards my own way of betterment and away from committing self-harm.

Since that initial ghostly experience, when I was around eight years old, I began to comprehend the reality of death and dying as mortal beings, and my mind began to open up its door to the world of spirit. The fact I was alone and a curiously minded child with very few friends afforded me the time to handle the concepts of spirituality with a mature understanding that I did not yet fully realise.

My experiences and training in mediumship began through a large amount of self-study and by practising on friends and acquaintances, long before I began holding sessions formally in a professional setting. I have a wonderful friend, Toni Reilly, to thank for encouraging me to take a huge leap of faith in believing in my own abilities. I had moved to Brisbane, and I was volunteering at Toni's stall during the busy Mind Body Spirit Festival. I was about nineteen years old at the time, and Toni knew I had a real interest in mediumship and in doing psychic work using Tarot cards. I wasn't confident in reading the cards for strangers, and Toni was aware of this. With that in mind, she literally grabbed a guy who was passing the stand and asked him if he wanted a Tarot reading with me. This put me on the spot; I was in shock, but I couldn't back out then. It was a successful sitting, my first ever paid professional reading, and Toni taught me to jump right in and swim. I owe it to her for that mindset, and I've now adopted it whenever I find myself hesitating with fear of failure. It was also Toni who first told me about finding a Spiritualist church in Brisbane, and she explained what they did there.

Brisbane still holds sentimentality for me, as it was there that I joined a spiritual development circle. With only a handful of these establishments left in Australia, the Spiritual Church Brisbane in Spring Hill was my first foray into sitting with spirit and learning the mechanics of mediumship. There I began to sit in the power of spirit, and I learnt to receive and give messages with constructive critique from my teacher. I also met a new group of like-minded friends to network with, people who loved the spiritual arts as much as I did. You can certainly study on your own for years, but it's always more fun with company.

I've since learnt that the majority of people who work as mediums have experienced death closely in their lives. Losing my mother when I was a young child burnt a brighter flame inside me to seek and uncover the goings-on of the mystery to the world on the other side. I wanted answers, but most of all I wanted to experience it for myself, and I needed to know if the human soul lived on. At the time I hadn't actively sought out a medium to connect with my mother; I did that a few years afterwards.

It wasn't until I was in my early twenties that I began to actually hold intuitive and mediumship readings for others. By that stage I had moved to Sydney, and my first mediumship reading was performed during a class break at the TAFE college where I was studying fashion design. My friend Elise and I were sitting outside in the food court, and we decided to test out my mediumship with a reading. It was my first lesson of clairsentience in mediumship, and I began to 'feel' an invisible yet almost electric energy build from above us. It travelled down slowly, and I felt them right beside me.

I remember feeling excited and shocked at the sensation as I described it out loud and in full detail to Elise. An experience like that one was excellent, as it gave a sense of authority to the situation and allowed me to open up fully to the moment, with complete trust. I closed my eyes and began to relay as much detail of the images and sensations that came through, and I sensed the spirit energy was the essence of her maternal grandfather. At the time some details came through that Elise couldn't confirm, but she later came to me in the following days excitedly relaying that her mother affirmed those very details. That was my moment of realisation and the beginning of the seed that would grow. It doesn't matter how you go into the session, other than in pure honesty with yourself and your sitter, right from the second you begin to the moment you finish the reading.

Being spiritually inclined since childhood, and living and working in mediumship and metaphysics have definitely shaped my emotional intelligence. I've been better able to process situations connected with death, spirituality and relationships. Navigating every problem regarding relationships or life in general is another matter, as we are still human, and experiencing human faults is imperative to our personal growth and emotional learning.

After a few years and an interstate move, I began assisting on the Rockpool Publishing stand at the Mind Body Spirit Festivals, selling books and cards at all of the various expos. Eventually, I joined Rockpool full-time and became a part of the small Sydney-based publishing house. My role was in sales and marketing, among wearing a number of other hats. During my time there, I developed three decks of cards myself, 'Pure Magic Oracle Cards', 'Divine Doors Oracle' and 'Saints and Mystics Reading Cards'.

I am a great advocate for continued and ongoing study of both mediumship and psychic abilities, but some schools and courses can be very expensive for a majority of people. I guess that's why it's so popular for most mediums to share similar paths of learning, anchored in firstly sitting in circle in spiritual groups. It's important to not be discouraged with mediumship, and when you make the commitment to learn to sit with spirit and to study this work, other doors do open up. It's important to learn from someone who knows how to teach well, and it's just as important to be patient in the journey.

I would highly recommend studying mediumship with any of these mediums: Louise Herman, Tony Stockwell, Christine Morgan, Travis Sanders, Charles Virtue, Debbie Malone and attending schools such as The Awareness Institute in Sydney and, of course, the well-known and highly respected Arthur Findlay College in the United Kingdom. One of the best lessons of advice I have been given was during a workshop with Louise Herman and Tony Stockwell in Sydney. Louise urged the group (I'm paraphrasing here) that the best mediumship comes from our own personal experiences with people. We learn so much through people, no matter their standing and whether they're homeless or wealthy, a family man or high-flying businesswoman. How can we expect to understand different signs from spirit if we don't expand on our spiritual dictionary through people in life?

I detached from my Catholic roots a long time ago, as I couldn't feel 'at home' in the structure of Christianity, though I did leave the system having learnt the importance of, and having a love for, the ritual of prayers and spirit veneration. It wasn't until I was in my adult years that I've grown towards different forms and paths of spirituality to decide what I actually wanted. I find great understanding and respect for many strands of religious practices, as many offer a legitimate path of constructing the spiritual in the mundane, with integrity and intelligence for the seeker, without a need to recruit or entice outsiders to join.

While I keep my religious path generally private, some good old practices have stayed. I still honour spirits and saints, I maintain dedicated rites and rituals on sacred days and ceremonial occasions and I keep an altar for my ancestral spirits, as I learn and work with them day to day. I believe in the power of spirits, the invisible, the mysteries and, quite certainly, angels and ancestors.

One of the biggest learning experiences I've received was during a reading that took place with a woman who spoke no English and wanted to link with her late husband. The sitting was held with at least three other people present in the room, as they were my point of translation. The messages that came through from the spirit communicator, her husband, were a great lesson in remembering how spirit works so beautifully in communicating love, without the barriers of language. While it was incredibly hard work to focus on interpreting the messages carefully, I managed to convey key words to a love song they had once shared with one another.

Another important memory during that same year was when my own mother came through to me for the very first time. I had moved to Melbourne and was having such a hard time settling in, so I began to meditate to help with my angst. I was in so deep that I was just about to fall asleep, then I envisioned myself immediately being transported to a room in a different house that I was not familiar with.

I was standing in a hallway with the kitchen door open in front of me. I heard a noise to my left and saw my mother walking through the front door of the house.

In all my years of readings and connecting, I have connected with other friends who have passed before and with spirits I've known through others in my life. Not once was I worried about not seeing my mother, as I knew in my heart the timing would come at the right moment. When I opened my eyes a while after, I found I had fallen asleep, and I sat up trying to take in what I had just felt and seen. I decided to go outside and sit in the sunshine, and immediately after walking through my own front door a massively large monarch butterfly appeared out of nowhere and landed on my shoulder. I was a crying mess for the next hour, but that butterfly was to me confirmation of the mediumship I had experienced.

Australia is a young and fairly conservative country, but its roots belong to the beautiful rich history and culture of the Aboriginal people, with their own ancestral spirits, rituals and sacred Dreamtime stories. When you learn deeply about the land you reside in and you begin to study the spirituality through the history of native people, you begin to draw a line of where your influences in mediumship come from. While the practices of modern spiritualism have histories in America and England, shamanic practices of mediumship have been practised in Indigenous communities long before the rise of modern humanity.

From what I've experienced in the many different cities and countries I've visited, I find that mediumship is generally received with curiosity or interest rather than disapproval. But the most incredible places of openness I've ever experienced weren't in Australia's Byron Bay or Glastonbury in the United Kingdom, but in New Orleans, Louisiana, in the United States. Not only is New Orleans a beautiful kaleidoscope of cultures, but its blend of spiritual practices also gives the city its unique footprint in the world. With practitioners of witchcraft, Buddhism, Christianity, folk magic, Haitian Vodou and even New Orleans–style Voodoo. It's an impressive feat to see the display of eccentric faces and styles dancing alongside each other in the city of jazz and conjure. That openness is like nothing I've ever seen before, and I immediately knew this place would be my future home to live and eventually die in, one day.

Mediums often lose friends because of their mediumship, but I first lost a big group of mates the moment I came clear about my sexuality when I was teenager. When that happened, I was truly devastated. These guys were my brothers, and they were there for me when my mother passed away, but in a small town it's easy to empathise with them on the possible insults and false insinuations they would have encountered from closed-minded people, let alone their own comfortability in understanding and accepting the concept of any label other than 'straight' at that age. I was already spiritually minded during that time, so I thought, 'Why not let it all out? I'm sexually fluid, I love men and women, I believe in spirits, I can read the Tarot and I'm not afraid to throw a punch if I have to!'

I can't imagine what the conversation would be like to address your spiritual beliefs to family, and I can only imagine how tough and heartbreaking it can be for some people. I have friends today who are curious about what I do, but they will fight me to the death in arguing that the spiritual and the supernatural are all bullshit. I still love them, and I accept their right to think that way. I don't believe in actively changing people's minds to prove a point or trying to convince people of experiences they aren't open to experience themselves. I'm lucky to have a close-knit group of selective friends who I can call family, and while only a few are spiritually attuned or excited to discuss the subject, all of them are supportive in their belief of my own passions, and for that I am terribly grateful.

Through my past experiences of spirits and mediumship, I no longer hold a fear of death, and I do think of my friends and loved ones in the scenario and how we would meet again in the great beyond. Death, from what I've come to learn, is an awakening back into another world, whose landscape we recognise on a soul level, where our loved ones reside and meet us through the transition from this world and theirs. It's not a geographical location that's layered atop of Earth but one that blends together into the cosmos of all creation, where each planet and exploding star plays a vital role. And we are a part of it all.

In 2020 I stayed in a hostel in Scotland as part of my United Kingdom adventure, which was cut short because of the Covid-19 pandemic. The old premises of the hostel used to be the original jail and courthouse of Edinburgh; it was located where a lot of the old city has been built on top of its former self. There are many areas still with underground vaults that were built during the 1700s, and many have been reputed to be haunted by ghosts of history's past. My hostel was one of the few in Edinburgh that not only has the abandoned vaults below but also the remains of what was a normal old street, known locally as the Lost Close.

The hostel has kept the original structure of the jail, and there are still rooms in the same format that are literally old jail cells from the original building. I made a new friend during my stay, and she said that in her room the lights flickered on and off by themselves, curtains moved on their own and she could hear whispering in her ear at night. Naturally, I later moved from my spectacular room with a view on the top floor to join her in the 'enchanted' area, located on the viewless lower ground!

What was particularly interesting was seeing how she talked herself into explaining away the experiences, though no logical explanation could be achieved. She seemed unable and unwilling to accept that spirits may have been present in her room. While these situations excite the thriller in me, I always speak to others about what I sense, from a place of calm education.

My focus in mediumship is in running courses, classes and circles for people to develop their own skills, through psychic and mediumship work, rather than providing one-on-one sittings. I'm a strong believer in emphasising grounded ethics, while conducting spiritual practices and making sure to eradicate any sort of fanciful dependency on spiritual work as being superior or exclusive. I enjoy teaching in small to medium sized groups and, as we know, similar to distance healing, psychic energies are not trapped in the physical laws of Earth, and so messages can be conveyed quite easily via Zoom, Facetime, Skype and Instagram, all of which make online learning not just convenient but extremely fun to do.

My work as an author has afforded me the opportunities to travel, both domestically and internationally, to the United Kingdom and America, attending festivals, expos and bookshops for talks, workshops and seminars on the subjects of spirituality and metaphysics. For that I am incredibly grateful, and I'm floored by the reception of people who have approached me to talk about their insights and experiences from using the Oracle cards I have created.

I no longer disregard my senses with the people who I let into my crazy little world. I work with spirits in my personal life, and I have come to love the simple acts of veneration and offerings to saints and spirits that help navigate the way I listen and act to the winds that constantly change. I have learnt that life and maturity has everything to do with my mediumship in the way I address my own heart, and the hearts of others, as well as the way I treat my intuition, with trust and faith.

Author and medium
Age, 32
Sydney, Australia

www.mrengracia.co
Instagram: @mrengracia

Chapter twenty

In closing

When I first asked my friends to share aspects of their own lives and experiences relating to their mediumship unfoldment, I had no idea what would be said or where it might lead. What stood out to me as a common denominator was the naturalness of everyone's unique pathway to mediumship. Some knew very early on that mediumship was within them; others discovered their ability later on in life, as I did, and for many it became a part of their lives quite organically. They were simply led towards it.

As much as it was not my intention to make this book an unauthorised advertisement for Arthur Findlay College, I cannot overlook the importance of learning how to use this special gift properly, and it is colleges such as this one that deserve the accolades they receive. Great education produces very good mediums. It is also essential to work continuously on your own personal development. This can be done through meditation, joining a development circle, journaling and reading. These factors are essential in developing properly as a medium, psychic or healer.

Having reached this page, I would like to believe that mediumship as a practice has been demystified in many ways for you. Mediumship is about healing, hope and the opportunity to be reconnected to a loved one in the spirit world. In my opinion there is no place for ridiculous hype or witchy-woo absurdities that too often surround this sacred and ancient form of communication. It is not mysterious; it is real, relevant and natural.

As human beings we are all different, and mediums are no exception. Mediums also have varying points of view and differing opinions on a multitude of subjects, and we are just as culturally, politically, sexually and socially diverse as the rest of society. What is different and identifiable about mediums as a collective is our purpose in life. We are here to be the bridge between the two worlds, and in doing so we provide healing for both the living and for those in spirit.

Mediums come from all walks of life. We have varying levels of education. Age is irrelevant, as is sex and sexual orientation. Country of origin means nothing, nor does financial worth or status in society. What is essential with all mediums is that a deep and innate sensitivity exists, because without this delicate awareness communication with those in spirit is impossible.

When Sam passed I was desperate to read books that talked about death in a way that gave me hope about his transition into the next phase of life, the afterlife. Everything I picked up was depressingly similar, and none properly discussed the continuum of life in another dimension. I wasn't interested in religious perspectives and publications; I wanted to read books written by real living people who had experienced a personal trauma parallel to my own.

I had to know where Sam had gone, for in my eyes he had to 'be' somewhere. My lifelong beliefs could comprehend nothing less. These types of books were virtually impossible to find, which is why I wrote my own. In many ways, Demystifying Mediumship is a natural extension of the first, but it goes deeper into the importance of my own mediumship discovery and the realisation I was not alone in taking that path.

Take from this book what you will. We all have free choice to think, act, believe and worship as we wish. But I do hope that it does invoke a little spark of 'what if' for all who read it, and that our combined words do truly strike a chord.

Dare to believe!

Endorsements

'At last a book that really captures the essence of demystifying the modern medium. In reading this book, you'll discover the broad range of mediumistic gifts that exist, the various professions that some left to pursue their mediumship and the unique path that many have taken to uncover their gifts.

Kerry's book does a wonderful job of showing that mediumship is a natural phenomenon that is based in love: the language that bridges our human world and the spirit world. If you are looking for healing and understanding in your quest to learn more about mediumship, this book is a must-read.'

Udoka Nwanna is a former litigation attorney and current law school professor who holds a BA in psychology and is a spiritual psychic medium, known as the 'Spiritual Blacksmith' (California, USA)

'For too long the assumption that science and spirituality do not mix has polarised many in my profession. I've worked as a doctor in major hospitals, private practice and in natural disaster situations, including the tsunami in Sri Lanka, Hurricane Katrina in the USA and the earthquake in Haiti.

My role as a doctor has been to heal both medically and emotionally, and when in disaster areas, helping survivors heal, included feeling their loved ones in spirit. Through this spiritual connection I was naturally able to channel their loved ones in spirit, giving them comfort and honouring those people who had passed over.

This is a no-nonsense book that explores, explains and shares the fascinating stories of other mediums and how they combine their natural mediumistic abilities with working in mainstream society. Kerry's goal was to demystify mediumship, and I believe that she has done just that.'

Dr Ellyn Shander, MD, has specialised in psychiatry for the last thirty-nine years and is also a spiritual medium (Connecticut, USA)

About the Author

Kerry Alderuccio is an Australian author, psychic medium and inspirational speaker. Kerry conducts private readings from her home in Fitzroy North in Melbourne, Australia, and is a regular guest presenter at the Mind Body Spirit Festivals in Melbourne and Sydney. She was a presenter for the entirety of season one on the Awake TV Network, which was broadcast weekly online from San Diego in the USA.

Kerry can be contacted at
kerry@kerryalderuccio.com

and bookings can be made at
www.kerryalderuccio.com

and on Facebook at
'Kerry Alderuccio – Medium and Author'.

CPSIA information can be obtained
at www.ICGtesting.com
Printed in the USA
LVHW051611131121
703258LV00018B/1597

9 780645 307207